Home Plays.

DRAMAS ❧ BOYS

A Series of Original Comedies,

COMPRISING

MALE CHARACTERS ONLY.

BY

MISS KEATING,

AUTHOR OF

" Dramas for the Drawing Room," " Plays for the Parlour,"
&c., &c.

THOMAS HAILES LACY,

89, STRAND,

(Opposite Southampton Street, Covent Garden Market,)

LONDON.

CONTENTS.

EXPLANATION OF THE STAGE DIRECTIONS.

The Actor is supposed to face the Audience.

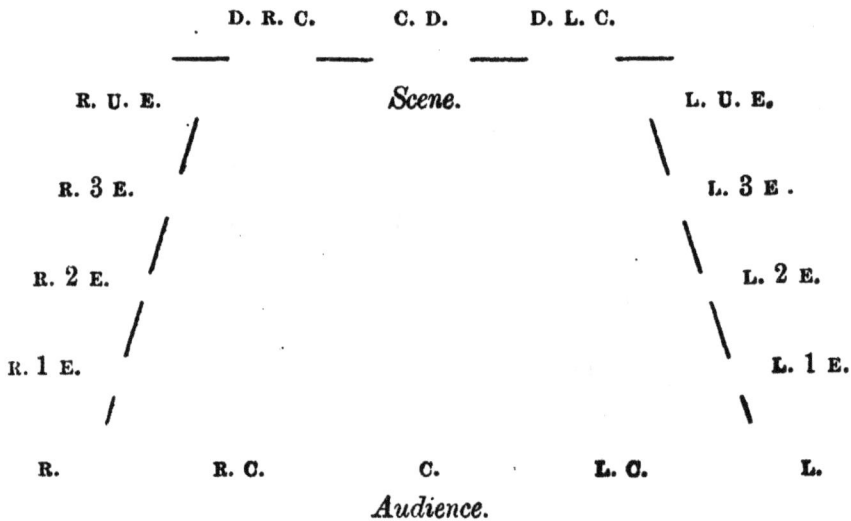

D. R. C.	C. D.	D. L. C.	

R. U. E.   *Scene.*   L. U. E.

R. 3 E.   L. 3 E.

R. 2 E.   L. 2 E.

R. 1 E.   L. 1 E.

R.   R. C.   C.   L. C.   L.

Audience.

L.	Left.	C.	Centre.
L. C.	Left Centre.	R.	Right.
L. 1 E.	Left First Entrance.	R. 1 E.	Right First Entrance.
L. 2 E.	Left Second Entrance.	R. 2 E.	Right Second Entrance.
L. 3 E.	Left Third Entrance.	R. 3 E.	Right Third Entrance.
L. U. E.	Left Upper Entrance (wherever the Scene may be.)	R. U. E.	Right Upper Entrance.
D. L. C.	Door Left Centre.	D. R. C.	Door Right Centre.

THE
PLOT OF POTZENTAUSEND.

𝔄 Comic Drama,

IN ONE ACT.

(FOR MALE CHARACTERS ONLY.)

THOMAS HAILES LACY,
89, STRAND,
(Opposite Southampton Street, Covent Garden Market,)
LONDON.

THE PLOT OF POTZENTAUSEND.

Characters.

GRINDSTONE (*a Miller—very* un*melodramatic, and by no means* " *A Jolly Miller* " ....

SACKS (*his Man, a benevolent-minded Hunchback*)

MAX (*a young Serjeant*) ....⎫

BERNARD (*a young Farmer*) .... ⎪ *(four trusting Swains, warranted harmless)*

LOUIS (*a Lawyer's Clerk*) ...... ⎬

FRITZ (*a young Peasant*) ...... ⎭

THE CHEVALIER D'ESPION (*a Man of Mystery*) ....

OFFICER ....

TWO GUARDS ....

The Scene is supposed to be in a Frontier Village in Germany.

Costumes—*later part of Louis XIV.'s Reign.*

GRINDSTONE. Brown long coat with short sleeves, long waistcoat, trunk breeches, grey stockings, grey hair, round broad-brimmed hat.

SACKS. Shirt sleeves, long red waistcoat, full breeches, grey stockings, shoes.

MAX. Blue long coat, faced with red, long white gaiters, white cravat, round hat with feather.

BERNARD. Round jacket, embroidered braces, full breeches, grey stockings, shoes.

LOUIS. Black long coat, waistcoat, and full breeches, black stockings, shoes.

FRITZ. A blue blouse, full breeches, blue stockings, shoes.

CHEVALIER. Gold-laced suit of the time, cloak, and hat trimmed with feathers.

OFFICER *and* SOLDIERS. Blue uniforms.

THE
PLOT OF POTZENTAUSEND.

SCENE.—*A Large Room in Grindstone's House. Practicable window,* L. C.; *large screen,* R.; *two doors,* R. *and* L.; *a table in centre; large high-backed chair, tall enough to hide any one behind it; smaller chairs, &c.; and stage dark.*

Enter SACKS, R., *with a small lighted lamp, which he places on table.*

SACKS. Well, of all the odd whims, did I ever hear of one like this! Here is my respected Master Grindstone, the best of millers (and I may add, the greatest rogue in grain,) for three miles round, forbidding the village lads and lasses to dance in his barn to-night—yes, actually considers it immoral; and instead of finishing up the yearly festival with a merry waltz, or a lively cotillion, he, as the magistrate's deputy, sends them all packing off at the last minute; orders their parents to keep them at home, safe under lock and key. Threatens to pillory the fiddlers, if they dare to scrape a string, or to shew their unlucky phizzes in the place. And as to merry making—lud a' mercy! he'll commit every soul to jail, who isn't in bed and snoring as the clock strikes nine. Why, the very dogs dare not bark nor an owl hoot without leave. Oh! here he comes. (*crosses to* R.)

Enter GRINDSTONE, *door* R. 1 E.

GRIND. Well, Sacks—have you been round the village and given my orders?

SACKS. Haven't I! to the very last tittle! And, la,

A 2

master! you should have seen the poor lasses, when I told them there was to be no dance to-night.

GRIND. What could the silly girls have to complain of, I should like to know? Haven't I treated them to an extra day's work in my orchard, and allowed them to appropriate to their own use all the apples they could pick up, that were not fit for use?

SACKS. That's quite true, master. But if you had heard what they said of you——

GRIND. Oh, indeed! And pray what was it they did say?

SACKS. Such things! First of all—little Ida, the cherry-cheeked daughter of one-eyed Blaize the inn-keeper—she comes bustling up, like a bantam hen with all her feathers ruffled—" So, Mr. Sacks," says she—for, bless you, she is so *polite* when she means to be very rude—" So, Mr. Sacks, your old fool of a master——"

GRIND. Did she presume to call me a fool? *Me?*— Grindstone, the magistrate's deputy! I'll take away her father's license. A fool, forsooth!

SACKS. Fool! was the very identical expression. But that is nothing to be shocked at, when she called *me* an ugly, spiteful hunchback. Well, but I haven't done! "Yes," says Rose, the tailor's niece—you know little Rose, the blue-eyed beauty, who boxed your ears for telling fibs of her sweetheart—"Tell Mr. Grindstone that we shall find a way to outwit him." "A sneaking old curmudgeon," says Julie. "A crabbed old bachelor," adds tall Mariette. "A regular rogue," adds Georgette. Ha, ha, ha! Oh! it was such fun to hear them all falling foul of you, and vowing they would break into the barn in spite of your teeth.

GRIND. Oh! ho! Will they?—we shall see. Of course, Sacks, you told them what to expect?—you made them understand what a terrible fellow I was?

SACKS. Of course I did, master. I said that a monster was a joke to *you*; "besides," says I "he has turned the fierce yard dog into the barn, and he'll kill the first that ventures in. You never saw such a quandary as they were in.

GRIND. Serve them right—a pack of saucy girls! Did you order the ferryman to take no one over, nor to bring anyone across, without an order from me?

Sacks. I did, master. So if the young ladies want to run away, they will have to walk two leagues round to the bridge, or else to wade through the ford. I offered to carry them across on my hump, provided they would each promise to have no partner but me the whole evening. Oh my! wasn't I abused! "Get rid of your hump!" says one—"You look like a travelling pedlar"—"Hadn't you better hire a monkey," says another, "and you two can shew yourselves for a penny a head"—"You would run easier on all fours"—"And just look at yourself in the glass." Oh!—I promise you I came in for my share of abuse, I did.

Grind. Serve you right, you old goose.

Sacks. Old goose! What next, I wonder.

Grind. No muttering, fellow; and mind, I am not at home to anyone to-night. You may shut the house up and go—

Sacks. Thank you, master.

Grind. To the deuce! or about your business;—hang, drown yourself, if you will—provided that you are at work by four in the morning.

Sacks. I'll do my best to oblige you;—good night, master. (*going*)

Grind. Stop, you may bring my hat and cloak, and the dark lanthorn. I am just going to take a turn in the village, and make sure that my orders have been punctually observed. (*Exit* Sacks, r.) That fellow is such a fool, he will never suspect that *I*, the honest old miller, should actually have a state secret in my keeping. I must have the place quiet, for at nine the chevalier will be here. Long ere that it will be pitch dark, and very favourable for the arrival of the other parties who are expected, and who are to find their way into this room by the old back entrance that is never used.

Enter Sacks *with hat, cloak, and lanthorn,* r.

Sacks. Here you are, sir—your hat (*gives hat*), your cloak, and your lanthorn. (*puts down lanthorn, and assists* Grindstone *to put on cloak*) Why, you look for all the world like a conspirator.

Grind. Conspirator!—you rascal! What do you mean? (*aside*) Can he suspect?

SACKS. I never mean anything, master. You know what a poor simple fellow I am.

GRIND. There—there—hold your tongue, and never let me hear you hint that a respectable miller, and a deputy magistrate, looks like a conspirator. I have a noble aim in view—a patriotic project. I shall increase my rheumatism, but add to my renown, by looking after the morals of the million.   *Exit with lanthorn*, L.

SACKS. Ah—ha, ha, ha! Simple as I seem, I am not to be blindfolded by you, Master Grindstone; and don't I know that morality would never send you out of a cold night. No, no, my good Grindstone—cunning as the fox may be, his skin comes to the currier at last. Well, as I have the place to myself, I shall obey orders—lock up the house, then return here, vote myself into the chair, and preside at a convivial meeting of one.

Exit with lamp, L.—*Music, " The winds whistle cold," played very piano and slowly.*

Enter BERNARD *from behind screen, which is supposed to conceal a door—Music ceases—he is wrapped in a cloak, and advances cautiously.*

BERN. What a cold walk I have had, two leagues round at least; so lonely, too; I did not meet a soul. Of course everybody is dancing in the barn. It is now the hour when Ida and her cousin appointed to meet me here. What a cross old fellow that Father Blaize is! he sees further with his one eye than I can with two, or else why should he forbid me to shew myself in his house. Never mind; my dear Ida and Georgette have promised to come here, and to remember to bring the supper. Hist! what footsteps are those? Clumpity—clumpity—clump. (*looks out at side, by which* SACKS *exits*) A man with a light— oh no—I shall hide—this screen is most convenient.

(*runs behind screen*)

Enter SACKS, L., *with lamp and basket.*

SACKS. Now to make a night of it. I have found a delicious pork pie, half a ham, and some beautiful cold roast pig; I hope there is variety for once in a way. Then here are eggs, cream, cheese, and a loaf of brown bread.

Exhausted nature may support herself on that till break-fast time to-morrow. Now then for the drinkables to give a zest to the grand banquet.

> (*puts basket and lamp on table, and exits,* R. BERNARD *peeps cautiously from behind screen—advances to table*)

BERN. Who is that accommodating gentleman with such an excellent appetite. It must be some benevolent friend of my little Ida, who compassionates a poor lover, and can feel for a hungry lad that has come out supperless. There can be no harm in appropriating this pie, which he so highly eulogised. I still leave him the ham and the cold pig. Bless me! he is actually returning, and Ida not here to introduce me—I must return to my hiding place. Suppose he should miss the pie, and look behind the screen. Surely there must be a closet of some kind—ah, here is one large enough to hold half a regiment. (*enters closet,* R.)

Re-enter SACKS, R. *door, with several bottles in another basket.*

SACKS. Here we are, all right; I can always find my way to the cellar in the dark; and somehow I know by instinct where the best vintage is stowed away. I shall now perform the part of a waiter, and commence by laying the cloth. (*puts down basket*) What a goose I am! I have forgotten the table cloth, plates, knives and forks, and when a gentleman invites himself to supper, he expects things to be done in a genteel way. The light is burning in the kitchen; I shall find what I want there. *Exit,* R.

> (*Music. "Let me like a soldier fall."* MAX *jumps in through window, he is in a serjeant's uniform, he comes forward*)

MAX. I am first at the place of rendezvous, which speaks well for my gallantry and punctuality, I have had a fine run for it—the old fool of a ferryman wanted to hinder me from passing over, because he said that he had received orders to do so; I soon settled that little matter, by pitching him out of his boat, and rowing myself over. I then secured the crazy old tub by a stout rope, so as to ensure my safe return to quarters before midnight. Rose and Georgette are very late, (*looks at table*) but they have made some preparation for supper, I perceive. A savoury ham! I may as well commence by attacking the commissariat. (*sits at table, pulls out a clasp knife, and begins eating*) If the young ladies don't appear soon, I very much doubt if there will be any of the supper left; it is vanishing with fearful rapidity. (SACKS *sings without*) What! is that a man's voice? it must be that crabbed old miller, who has slipped away from the barn— I mean the ball room, and most likely I am devouring his supper. (*rises*) So, Max, my friend, I advise you to lie in ambush for a while; the screen is the first place people look behind, this high-backed chair will make a capital barrier. (*places high backed chair near window*) But lest the garrison should be starved into a surrender, I shall carefully victual the citadel.

> (*takes off the ham, loaf, and bottle, and hides behind the large chair*)

Enter SACKS, R. *with a tray on which are plates, glasses, &c.*

SACKS. Now to lay the cloth. (*removes baskets from table, then spreads a large cloth over it*) Plates for four— there you are—dishes, glasses, bread—where's the bread? I could have sworn that I had brought in a loaf; what a cannibal I must have been, to have forgotten the bread; I'll get it directly, of course it is in the kitchen. *Exit,* R.

MAX. (*peeping from behind chair*) He never suspected who was listening to him. I wish these little girls would come; I shall be tired of playing at hide and seek, and if they delay much longer, I shall take the liberty of introducing myself to the party with the hump, and proposing that we commence supper without further delay. Footsteps again! (*listens*) This time it must be Rose and Georgette, and perhaps accompanied by one or two of their friends, the more the merrier; we shall be able to extemporise a ball here. (*listens again*) I'll hide, and just startle them on their appearance.

> (*conceals himself behind chair.—Music. "There's some one in the house with Dinah."*)

Enter LOUIS, *from window, followed by* FRITZ, *who carries a basket.*

LOUIS. (*advances*) It is all right, Fritz—we are safe now. That must have been old Grindstone that we dodged through the coppice.

FRITZ. I never was more frightened in my life; I'm sure that my heart was fairly down in the heel of my shoe, as one may say. Why, bless me! good gracious! oh la! did one ever!

LOUIS. Don't be a fool, little Fritz. What are you " Oh, la-ing !" and " Good gracious-ing !" about?

FRITZ. Just look at that table—all higgledy-piggledy, as one may say. There's a funny way to lay a cloth for supper.

LOUIS. As we have brought a good basketful of provender with us, suppose that we proceed to put everything in order, before Julie and Mariette come. Poor girls! if dancing has made them half as hungry as my long walk has made me, they will not be long before they appear in court. Come, Fritz, be quick, or we shall not be ready before the ladies arrive.

FRITZ. Now don't hurry a body, as one may say—I do not like it; in fact, I violently object to all such hasty proceedings. (*they bustle about, and arrange the table*)

LOUIS. What did you bring in that basket, Fritz ?

FRITZ. A cold goose, some sausages, and an apple tart; two bottles of cider, and a dish of plums. Here they are ! (*takes out dishes and arranges them on table*)

LOUIS. (*stumbles over* SACKS' *basket*) Why who could have brought this ?—Cold pig ! cheese !

FRITZ. Our sweethearts, of course. How thoughtful of the dear creatures! That cold pig, I must observe, looks very relishing, as a body may say.

LOUIS. One can scarcely ascertain that fact without previously tasting it. Suppose that we——

FRITZ. Sit down, and just try what it is like. I am quite of your opinion, Mr. Louis. (*they sit at table, and begin eating*)

LOUIS. It would be a pity to disarrange the table, or I should have suggested an attack on the goose. We will give the little girls ten minutes' grace, and then——

FRITZ. (*speaking with his mouth full*) Then we'll commence supper in earnest.

(BERNARD *peeps from closet, exclaims very loudly "Ahem!" and pops in again*)

LOUIS. What are you aheming about, Fritz?

FRITZ. Me ahem! I didn't ahem, as one may say.

LOUIS. Don't do it again; it startles me so.

MAX. (*looking over back of chair*) What are you doing there? (*disappears behind chair*)

FRITZ. Eh—was that you, Louis?

LOUIS. Me?—no! What was it? (*they rise*)

FRITZ. This isn't pleasant, as one may say. I begin to think, Louis, there's some one hid somewhere, as one may say.

LOUIS. (*listens*) Hush, do! There's some one coming. Quick—hide under the table—we shall be concealed there.

FRITZ. And at the same time I'll finish off the cold pig.

(*they both creep under the table, the cloth of which should touch the ground on all sides*)

Re-enter SACKS, *with a loaf,* R.

SACKS. At last I have found a loaf; and now I suppose I shall be allowed to begin supper. (*puts loaf on table*) My conscience! what does all this mean? I have a vivid recollection that I brought in sundry savoury preparations of pork, which I find transformed (*examines dishes*) into roast goose, tart, and plums. I haven't been walking in my sleep; I am not dozing; I don't see double. (*pinches his arm*) I feel that; and physically, if not morally, I am wide awake. Who can it be that has so politely secured this second repast. Hallo! here's more hocus-pocus work. Somebody—I name no names, so I can't give offence—but I wish merely to hint that some one has feloniously decamped with some one else's property, leaving this in exchange. Here are my baskets emptied—positively emptied. That's cool! I shall at once confiscate the deposit. First let me ascertain that all is right. (*Music—*SACKS *looks behind screen, closes window, and draws the curtain—whilst his back is turned,* LOUIS *and* FRITZ *come from under the table, remove all the dishes, and hide behind screen—*SACKS, *advancing with great pom-*

posity) Mr. Sacks, may I request the honour of your company to supper? (*bows*) Sir, I shall feel delighted. (*bowing*) Mr. Sacks, allow me to conduct you to the head of the table. (*bows*) With the greatest pleasure, sir. (*bows*) After you, sir. (*bows*) Oh, sir, you are too polite.

> (*as he turns up stage, the four* YOUNG MEN *disappear into their several hiding places—*SACKS *seats himself at the head of the table*)

SACKS. Now, my good friend Sacks—eh! oh! (*starts up*) This is too bad! the goose is gone. (*comes to front*) I'm not naturally pusillanimous, but hang it, this is carrying the joke too far, as well as the goose. (*exclaims*) Who is that? Don't be a fool! I know where you are! under the table. I wish I had courage to look round.

> (*During this speech* SACKS *faces the audience, and* FRITZ, LOUIS, MAX, *and* BERNARD *bring back the remainder of the supper, place it on the table, and seat themselves, two on either side, leaving the high-backed chair at the head for* SACKS)

What is that? I certainly heard a noise! it's the cat, of course, it is sure to be the cat. Here, puss! puss! pussy! pussy! (*turns round and perceives the young men, staggers to side*) Oh, my conscience! I feel as if I was a going to go. (YOUNG MEN *laugh*) Oh please don't; consider my nerves. (*they all four rise and run to* SACKS, *who snatches up a chair to defend himself*) Keep off, I'm a desperate fellow! I nearly shot a man one day, only the gun wasn't loaded, and didn't go off.

BERN. Is it possible, Sacks, that you do not recognize me, your old friend Bernard?

MAX. And I, corporal Max, with whom you have smoked many a pipe?

LOUIS. Surely you recollect me, Louis, clerk to worthy Herr von Botherman—the old rascal!

FRITZ. You won't pretend to say that I'm not your own loving cousin Fritz?

SACKS. (*putting down the chair*) Well, now I look at you a little closer, you are not such rogues as I took you for. But what brings you here in Master Grindstone's mill, at this hour of the night?

MAT. (*slapping him on the shoulder*) To meet our sweethearts, who appointed this place of rendezvous.

BERN. And who intend to slip away from the dancers in the barn, where, alas! we poor lads are forbidden to shew ourselves.

SACKS. (*laughing*) Ho, ho, ho! So you came to meet your sweethearts? Poor dear deluded boys! I regret to say that you will all be terribly disappointed. I've an idea the young ladies don't intend to come.

LOUIS. How is that? Explain!

ALL. Yes, yes—explain if you can.

SACKS. Now don't lose your tempers, young gentlemen; but the fact is, that for some reason or other, my excellent master, Grindstone, the magistrate's deputy, has forbidden the dance to take place to-night, and has commanded all the papas and mammas to lock up their beloved daughters, which must account for their non-appearance.

FRITZ. What a shame! and I brought a beautiful goose.

SACKS. Don't let the memory of the goose affect you, cousin Fritz. I see that you have prepared a snug supper. Suppose that we sit down to it, and thus console ourselves for the absence of the young ladies.

BERN. Well, I consent; but every mouthful I eat of the goose will remind me of my dear Ida.

MAX. Nonsense, man! I vote for supper instanter, and little Sacks shall be president.

ALL. Agreed! Agreed!

SACKS. If you insist on it, I'm agreeable; so we'll stand on no ceremony, but fall to at once. (*they all sit at table,* SACKS *in the tall chair at head, and begin eating*) Really, considering all things, we are as well off here as in the barn.

MAX. I am of your opinion, Sacks, though my little Georgette is perhaps breaking her heart.

BERN. And poor Ida—just fancy her despair.

SACKS. I don't fancy anything of the kind, particularly after the scolding they all gave me. But to prove that I bear no malice, I'll propose a toast. Here's to the ladies, or if you like it better, here's to the young ladies.

ALL. Here's to the young ladies! Well done, Sacks!

SACKS. I would on this occasion, gentlemen, make a

speech, only there happens to be nothing to make a speech about. (*a loud whistle is heard*) Hark! what is that? Who is that whistling? (*they all rise*) It sounds exactly like Master Grindstone's whistle. I should know it among a thousand. Now be quiet, all of you, boys, whilst I run out and look about me. *Exit,* L.

LOUIS. Why, who can it be?

FRITZ. Good gracious; is there any danger?

MAX. Danger, you little poltroon! Not whilst *I* am here to defend you.

BERN. Yes, you young gosling, what are you frightened at, I should like to know?

Re-enter SACKS, *hurriedly*, L.

SACKS. Run, run and hide, every man jack of you, or you will be in a fearful scrape.

MAX. What's the matter, Sacks?

SACKS. Matter enough! Master Grindstone has returned, but who he can be whistling to I don't know. He'll be sure to come here.

ALL. What will become of us?

MAX. Hide us somewhere, do.

SACKS. Hush—keep your senses about you. First clear away these things, then till the place is clear again, hide yourselves anywhere.

> *Music, "Oh dear, what can the matter be." They all bustle about, stow away the supper in the closet, into which* MAX *and* BERNARD *enter, and slam the door in the face of* FRITZ *and* LOUIS, *who also run to it. The two last hide under the table, and* SACKS *blows out the candle, and hides behind the window curtain. Very melodramatic music.*

Enter GRINDSTONE, *in long cloak, with a dark lanthorn,* L.—*he lights the candle on table, and then looks cautiously round.*

GRIND. Good! All is quiet—not a soul here. (SACKS *peeps from behind curtain*) That rogue, Sacks, I am thankful to say, is out of the way—snoring in his cock-loft—I heard him as I came in. Now to let in the Chevalier. (SACKS *disappears behind curtains*—GRINDSTONE *goes on tiptoe behind screen, claps his hands three times, and returns*) That is the signal agreed on: it is to signify that all is safe, and that he may enter by the old passage.

Enter CHEVALIER D'ESPION, *from behind screen, he also wears a large cloak, and a slouched hat.*

CHEV. Is all safe?

GRIND. Not so much as a mouse stirring, on the honour of an honest miller. (*bows*)

CHEV. An honest miller! Well, that is a novelty now-a-days. But I am afraid Master Grindstone that you have been overparticular, and had the ferry boat secured on the wrong side of the river. Of course you do not guess —in fact you do not know anything at all of the business that brings me here to night.

GRIND. Nothing, your **excellency**, but what you are pleased that I should know.

CHEV. It will be better for you to remain in perfect ignorance of this little affair; so remember that you forget everything connected with it.

GRIND. I will be deaf, dumb, and even blind, if your excellent Excellency wishes it.

CHEV. Exactly what I do wish; let this be a sign, that I appreciate your great zeal. (*gives a purse*) Retire now; keep watch; and should any unpleasant intruders demand admittance here in the name of the law, give the signal whistle—and then——

GRIND. Knock them down, my lord!

CHEV. No, admit them, and tell them as many false-hoods as you conveniently can call to mind. I shall take care of myself. Leave me—and hark you—as you value your ears, keep out of earshot, and watch the outer entry.

GRIND. I shall obey your orders, most illustrious sir.

Exit door, R.

CHEV. The success of this plot will make the fortune of my illustrious patron; and should we be interrupted I have taken my measures so well, that detection is next to an impossibility. Where have my confederates concealed themselves so effectually? for I know they have arrived, I watched their entrance from my hiding place. This closet for instance—(*opens closet door, and discovers* MAX *and* BERNARD) Enter, gentlemen, our other friends are here no doubt.

MAX. Our other friends! we are only two harmless lads, I asssure you, sir.

CHEV. Yes, yes, I understand; you are perfectly right. A corporal in the regiment near Potzentausend, and your companion there, an honest young farmer.

BERN. (*aside to* MAX) He knows us!

CHEV. This table shelters two others, perhaps. (*moves aside table—discovers* FRITZ *and* LOUIS, *who scramble to their feet*) Admirably managed! a peasant boy, and one of the learned profession; your disguise is excellent.

FRITZ. (*aside to* LOUIS) We are found out, as one may say.

LOUIS. (*to* FRITZ) Mum! not a word! Keep your own counsel.

CHEV. There is—or ought to be a fifth. Ah! ha! That curtain, I did not perceive it. (*draws aside curtain, and discovers* SACKS) We only wait for you, sir, to commence the conference.

SACKS. Goodness me! I'm getting into a scrape, I'm thinking.

CHEV. We had better be seated. I will preside, and hear the report of each in succession. (*the* CHEVALIER *seats himself at the head of table in the high-backed chair, the four young* MEN *sit, two on either side—and* SACKS *brings forward an old stool, and seats himself* R. *of table*) Now, gentlemen, as caution is necessary, even among friends. I shall mention no one by name. I will first address my neighbour, the corporal——

MAX. Corporal Max, so please you, of the Potzentausend Chasseurs, absent on leave.

CHEV. Exactly so! you have learnt your lesson I see. Then, as a military man, and doubtless renowned for politeness and gallantry, you will know who is meant by the "Fair Lady." What is your opinion of her conduct? Has she kept her word?

MAX. Well, I can't say that she has, and I begin to fear——

CHEV. Ha! what!—speak!

MAX. That she is playing me false with a rival. (*aside*)

Now Miss Ida, if that fellow is making up to you, he has a bit of my mind.

CHEV. (*making a note in pocket book.*) Then it is as we feared—the Marchioness will betray Austria. That Pompadour is a very Machiavelli. (*to* BERTRAND) You represent the Agricultural interests: what says the Farmer? Is he satisfied?

BERN. Not he! Grumbles as much as ever—talks of lowering the wages—complains of the scarcity of wool——

CHEV. (*aside*) Worse still—the Farmer-General against us; after being been allowed to fleece the nation. Where shall we get money for the secret service? (*to* LOUIS) Surely you have better news. What will the Law do on the occasion? You know to what I allude, the great case now pending.

LOUIS. (*aside*) I don't know anything of the kind but I'll say something at a venture. Oh—ah—yes—well—I think we shall win the day.

CHEV. Indeed! That makes amends for all! (*aside*) If the Chancellor is our friend, we can make head against the rest. (*to* FRITZ) As the deputy from the rural interests, that is the country people, what is your opinion?

FRITZ. Well, sir, my opinion is that provided you treat them well they are all right.

CHEV. Admirably, and wisely expressed. (*aside, making note*) Ripe for revolt, but we must be liberal in bribes, and promises. (*to* FRITZ) I look upon you, friend, as a great moral philosopher.

FRITZ. Oh don't, sir,—I do assure you, I'm one of the honestest, hard-workingest boys in the province, as one may say.

CHEV. Your zeal is appreciated. (*to* SACKS) Now my hitherto silent, and discreet friend.

SACKS. (*aside*) Ah! I thought he wouldn't forget me. Now for it.

(CHEVALIER *rises, approaches* SACKS, *who jumps up and retreats as the other advances.*)

CHEV. (*aside to* SACKS) Fear nothing—I know all.

SACKS. Really now! Well that is wonderful: what all about the goose, and cold pig, and the wine?

CHEV. Hush! caution! those at the table know literally nothing at all of the grand plan.

Sacks. Plan! what plan?

Chev. That which the illustrious Saxe has submitted to notice.

Sacks. (*aside*) The illustrious Sacks! That is meant for me.

Chev. I recognise in you his envoy—the only man fit to be trusted. Tell him the mill is in danger; he will know to what I allude.

Sacks. The mill in danger. Had I not better run and tell master Grindstone? (*a loud whistle is heard*) Eh, what is that. (Bernard, Max, Louis, *and* Fritz *start up*)

Chev. It means that we are surprised: that signal is my warning. (*noise within*) Ha! they approach. But be under no apprehension, either on your account, or mine; and recollect to keep up the character you have assumed —that of five young fellows who have met here to have a little private merry-making.

Sacks. Well, and so we are—five honest lads.

Chev. Our next interview will be decisive. Be cautious in your replies. Farewell—my path lies here.

Exit behind screen.

Sacks. It strikes me, boys, that we shall be in a hobble, if we are found out; so let us all hide—I hear Grindstone coming.

All. Yes, yes—let us hide.

Sacks. And if we are discovered, leave everything to me—I will get you off. Run into the closet, all of you!

(*the four* Young Men *hide in closet*, Fritz *attempts to enter first, but is put aside by* Max, Louis, *and* Bernard *follow* Max, *and finally* Fritz *goes in*)

Sacks. (*listens*) Yes—they are coming. Master Grindstone is talking pretty loud too. Well, I've done nothing! So here I'll sit. Walk in, gentlemen, as soon as you please. (*sits on stool near table, and slouches his hat over his face*)

Enter Grindstone, Officer, *and* Two Soldiers, L.

Grind. You can search the house if you choose, sir, and begin by this room.

Officer. (*to* Soldiers) Secure the door, and shoot the

B

first man that attempts to escape. (*perceives* SACKS) A man here!

GRIND. I assure you, captain, on the word of an honest miller, I know not who it can be.

OFFIC. (*to* SACKS) Speak, fellow—who are you?

SACKS. (*rising*) Please, noble captain, I am only Sacks.

OFFIC. Sacks! and in the name of wonder, who is Sacks?

SACKS. I am only Sacks—master Grindstone's man.

OFFIC. You have had accomplices, villain!

SACKS. (*looking at* GRINDSTONE) Yes, I confess—there have been persons here—that—that I would rather not betray.

OFFIC. (*holding his sword to* SACKS' *throat*) Instantly confess that you have been concealed in this room.

GRIND. Yes, rascal, confess! (*aside*) I'll lay all the blame on him.

SACKS. I will if you will remove your sword.

OFFICER. Well, there—proceed!

SACKS. (*looking at* GRINDSTONE) I was concealed behind the curtain.

OFFICER. And the others, your companions?

SACKS. Were also hidden in the room.

OFFICER. (*to* SOLDIERS) Search for them! (OFFICER *walks up to window*—SOLDIERS *search behind screen, under table*)

SACKS. (*aside to* GRINDSTONE) I say, master! I know all. But just confirm the truth of what I confess, and you shall come off with flying colours. (*to* OFFICER *who comes forward*) Most noble captain, you and your men of valour may save yourselves all further trouble, by just peeping into yonder closet.

OFFICER. A closet! Oh ho! (*opens the door suddenly* FRITZ *tumbles out—he collars him*) Now young man, who are you? and what brings you here?

FRITZ. Please, I am only Fritz, farmer Hildberg's boy; a harmless lad, as one may say.

OFFICER. (*throwing him off*) A harmless lad indeed! And who are these? (*goes to closet, and drags out* LOUIS, MAX, *and* BERNARD *follow*) Pray who are these fellows? (*perceives* MAX) What do I see? Max, my young corporal, among the conspirators! How is this, Max? Why are you here?

MAT. (*salutes à la militaire*) Absent on leave, captain.

OFFICER. And who are your companions?

GRIND. Yes, fellow, who are they? Why, as I live I declare they are only Bernard and Louis. Captain, I told you it was all a mistake; bless you, there are no conspirators here, I know every one of them.

SACKS. If you, noble captain, will allow me, I can explain everything. You see, sir, to-night was to have been the conclusion of the village fête, when all the lads and lasses were to have finished the revels, by a dance in Master Grindstone's barn; and these four young gentlemen came for the purpose of seeing their sweethearts, who had promised to meet, and sup with them here. (*aside to* GRINDSTONE) Now don't you contradict me, or I'll betray the secret.

OFFICER. Well, Sacks, proceed.

SACKS. So, captain, as for some reason or other the dance was postponed, my young friends would not be disappointed; so they determined to have supper, and we were enjoying ourselves very much, when you interrupted us.

OFFICER. A very plausible story; but who will vouch for the truth of it?

SACKS. (*runs to closet, brings out the supper, holds up the goose*) Behold my proofs! You must know, captain, that Fritz, my rural friend, not thinking his own company sufficient, brought another goose to keep him in countenance. (OMNES *laugh*) And as to the little disappointment touching the ball, Master Grindstone intends to put that all to rights—don't you, master?

GRIND. To be sure I do.

SACKS. He only put it off in order to do the thing handsomely; so he means to have a famous ball and supper to-morrow night, to which he invites you, sir, and moreover, he has in his pocket a certain purse——

OFFICER. A purse!

SACKS. The contents of which he intends to distribute among the young folks to buy them all fairings.

GRIND. (*aside to* SACKS) You villain!

SACKS. Not another grumble! Out with the purse, master.

GRIND. (*gives purse to* SACKS) Here it is, captain— exactly as Sacks has told you.

OFFICER. And as we have really discovered nothing, I presume there is nothing to discover. The Chevalier d'Espion, whom I came to arrest, is certainly not here.

SACKS. Most decidedly he is not, captain—and thus ends THE PLOT OF POTZENTAUSEND.

(*the Curtain drops to the Air of " Over the Sea*")

INCOG;

OR,

"FINE FEATHERS MAKE FINE BIRDS."

An original Farce,

IN ONE ACT.

———

FOR MALE CHARACTERS ONLY.

———

THOMAS HAILES LACY,

89, STRAND,

(*Opposite Southampton Street, Covent Garden Market,*)

LONDON.

Characters.

MONSIEUR CANNELLE (*a Grocer—ex-Mayor of Courville* ....

MONSIEUR LE DOUX (*Confectioner, and Marquillier or Churchwarden*) ....

MONSIEUR LE BLANC (*Perfumer*) ....

BARBEAU (*Landlord of the " Golden Goose"*)

PICARD (*his Man-Servant*) ....

EUGENE
MARCEL } (*young Travellers*) ....{

➤➤➤➤➤ ❖ ◄◄◄◄◄

Scene.—IN A SMALL FRENCH TOWN.

TIME.—LOUIS XV.

COSTUMES OF 1770.

CANNELLE.—Red cloth coat, silk waistcoat, red breeches, white stockings, shoes and buckles, white cravat, powdered wig, and a three-cornered gold laced hat.

LE DOUX.—Light cloth or silk coat, light waistcoat, black silk breeches, white stockings, shoes and buckles, white cravat, wig and powder, and three-cornered hat.

LE BLANC.—Blue cloth coat, nankeen waistcoat and breeches, striped stockings, shoes and buckles, three-cornered hat, and powder.

BARBEAU.—Plain brown coat with metal buttons, white waistcoat, black breeches, white stockings, white cravat, and long hair tied in queue.

PICARD.—Shirt sleeves, red waistcoat, brown cloth breeches, grey stockings, shoes, apron, and red cap.

EUGENE.—Green riding coat with cape, top boots, white breeches, white cravat, powdered wig, and gold laced three-cornered hat. *Second Dress:* Same as Marcel's suit.

MARCEL.—His dress is described in page 15. *Second Dress:* Plain suit.

INCOG.

SCENE.—*A large Room in the "Golden Goose," on the ground floor; window in back, through which the distant country is seen; doors,* R. 1 E., L. 1 E., *and* L. 3 E.; *fireplace,* L. 2 E.; *table, chairs, &c.*

Enter BARBEAU *and* CANNELLE, *door,* L. 1 E.

BARBEAU. This is indeed extraordinary, Monsieur the Mayor—*ex*-mayor, I mean! What, our old landlord, the Marquis of Courville is dead at last?

CANNELLE. Very dead indeed, neighbour; and he has done our village cemetery the honour of being buried there.

BARB. Dear me! that will not do us much good. So he is dead? I really thought he intended to live to the age of Methusalem, poor old fellow!

CANNEL. Old fellow! Is that the mode, Barbeau, in which you name departed nobility? in which you speak of the lamented deceased, Alexander Julius Cæsar Antony Augustus de Courville, Seigneur of the village?—I'm petrified! It is too much for my philosophy!

BARB. I meant no offence, Monsieur Cannelle; I was merely about to observe——

CANNEL. Observe it then with more deference to departed dignity! Well, you were going to observe?

BARB. That as the old—I mean the venerable Marquis —never was married, he cannot have left any heirs. Now, who think you, will succeed to the property?

CANNEL. Friend Barbeau, in this province, it does not become individuals to be curious. Suffice it to be known, there *is* a successor—a cousin.

BARB. Morbleu! There's **a** *successor!* Perhaps——

CANNEL. Not a bit of it. It is no *perhaps*; it is, I may say, a decided fact—a certainty. So this successor, when

A 2

he appears, will be received with due honours, by a loyal and devoted tenantry.

BARB. And when is the gentleman—the successor, the heir coming?

CANNEL. Parbleu! I do not mind telling you, Barbeau, that he may arrive at any moment.

BARB. But after all, who is he? What is his name?

CANNEL. Hush! hush! (*looks around, cautiously*) I do not object letting you into a secret, Barbeau; his name is for the present a mystery.

BARB. A what?

CANNEL. A mystery—that is, he does not wish anyone to know anything about him.

BARB. Good! And does he not in his letters to you, Monsieur the Mayor, ex-mayor I mean—does he not mention the time of his arrival? For of course he will alight here, the chateau being in a most tumble-down condition.

CANNEL. A tumble-down condition! Was there ever a more disrespectful epithet applied to an ancient feudal residence?—to the Chateau de Courville, the most pic-turresque ruin, I mean edifice, in the province.

BARB. Picturesque, if you please! Only half the rooms have no ceilings, and the rest of them no floors. I was about to observe, with all due deference to the chateau, that I suppose Monsieur the Marquis will take up his quarters here at the "Golden Goose." When you do write to him, Monsieur Cannelle, you can just hint that my hotel is the only hotel in the town worthy of being called an hotel. And although the Silver Lion pretends to a great deal, it is not fit to hold a candle to the "Golden Goose." Only just put in a good word for me, and I shall be one of your best customers.

CANNEL. So I would, Barbeau, only, between friends, the heir has not written to any one, not even to old Babette, the concierge of the chateau. I have heard that he intends to steal a march on us. He travels incog.

BARB. Ah! he travels incog. Is that any new-fangled sort of a carriage?

CANNEL. Barbeau, your ignorance shocks me. I blush for you. Learn, sir, that incog. means—it means——

BARB. Ah! it means?

CANNEL. Exactly so; it means—incog!

BARB. Wonderful!

CANNEL. He has left Paris, and it is supposed for this village; but nobody is to know anything about it, so—mum!—you understand?

BARB. Perfectly! But if monsieur the heir has any *nouse*——

CANNEL. Nouse! What a barbarism! Barbeau, as if a great nobleman could want *nouse*! It is all very well for the cannaille, who have to work for their bread, but great noblemen are not obliged to be at the trouble of thinking.

BARB. Pardon me, I was only going to observe, that the gentleman is sure to select my house: so I shall begin to bustle about, and get the best room ready. Oh, dear me, how very unfortunate! my best bed room——

CANNEL. It has not been stolen, I presume?

BARB. No; but I have let it to that young gentleman who came here two days, and is a stranger to these parts.

CANNEL. How is this, Barbeau? A stranger here, and *I* not yet informed of his appearance! Who knows what he may be?

BARB. You were out of the way, Monsieur Cannelle, and as you are—pardon me—*ex*-mayor——

CANNEL. Never mind that, friend Barbeau.

BARB. And as his passport was all right, it was no business of mine to enquire who he was.

CANNEL. But there are ways of ascertaining; there is perhaps a name on his valise; he has papers.

BARB. Not a scrap; and he came from somewhere on foot, carrying a small portmanteau, so securely locked, it would puzzle the Paris police to make anything out of it. Besides, the mayor, with whom he had an interview, appears satisfied. He pays regularly. *I* am satisfied, and—bless me! I think that must be the young gentleman himself—here he comes.

(EUGENE *is seen passing the window*, L. *to* R.)

CANNEL. Why, surely, I have met that young man before. He goes roving about the country making sketches, taking long walks, and giving remarkably short answers when addressed by any one.   But I shall ferret out who he is.

BARB. As you please, monsieur the *ex*-mayor ; but be discreet, if you please, for he is a good customer, and I cannot afford to affront him.

CANNEL. Offend him !—certainly not ; but I suspect there is something suspicious about this young stranger. So, Barbeau, I shall just step into the next room, and take counsel with myself as to what is to be done respecting him.   *Exit, door* L. 1 E.

BARB. A meddling old noodle ! What business is it of his ?   Yet, I confess, I also have *my* suspicions.

Enter EUGENE *from door*, R. ; *he is very plainly dressed in the fashion of the times, hair powdered, but he wears no sword, and his costume should be that of a traveller —boots, overcoat, &c.*

EUGENE. (*to* BARBEAU *who advances*, L.) Ha, landlord, good morning ! What can I have for breakfast ? The air of these hills gives a famous appetite, and seems to produce nothing else.

BARB. Oh, monsieur, you do us injustice ; the country round Courville is most fertile.

EUGENE. Ah, I forgot ! It certainly boasts of the greatest variety and abundance of thistles and dandelions, and the largest jack-asses I ever beheld, I should say that their progenitors must have been the aborigines of the place ; no offence, Barbeau, to the two-legged animals who now form the population. But apropos, of breakfast.

BARB. In less than five minutes, I promise you a first rate cutlet, a fricassee of rabbit, and such coffee !

, EUGENE. Capital ! I have great faith in your cutlets, but the last fricandeau of rabbit was rather suspicious ; I fear, Barbeau, that when alive those rabbits used to hunt mice and mew.

BARB. (*expostulating*) Oh! now really, monsieur, on the honour of an innkeeper !

EUGENE. And to say nothing disparaging of the coffee, it flavours more of the bean, than of the berry ; all very judicious were I a horse, but as I go on two legs, I prefer biped's food. Now make haste, and let me have breakfast as soon as possible.

BARB. You shall be served directly. (*aside*) So, he suspects my rabbits of being cats! Well, my young gentleman shall have his joke, and *pay* for it.

Exit door, L. 1 E.

EUGENE. (*throws his hat on table*) How provoking it is that I can discover no trace of this man, who seems to have disappeared at the same time that my only parent was forced from her home and child! The old concierge, at the ruined chateau, can tell me nothing, or, what is much the same, *will* tell me nothing: and my clever acute notary, Monsieur Vichy, is equally in the dark—yet we have discovered that a domestic, named Phillipe, was in the confidence of the late Marquis, whether he be living or dead, we cannot ascertain. What a foundation for a grand romance my early history would furnish!—An orphan— so very interesting, that—educated, and liberally supplied with funds by an unknown benefactor,—how terribly mysterious! But suddenly the supplies cease; and, one never-to-be-forgotten day, an ominous-looking letter, with a black seal, rivalling in size a crown piece, informs me that I am nobody, and have nothing—remarkably pleasant that piece of intelligence. But as a remedy to this ill-luck, a good-natured notary, of whom I had never heard, suddenly appears on the scene, as appropriately as the fairy godmother in the story book, and informs me that I am——

Enter CANNELLE *from door*, L.

CANNEL. (*speaking as he enters*) Never mind, Barbeau, I will wait here. (*affects surprise at seeing* EUGENE) Ah! I beg pardon, Monsieur; I hope that I am not intruding.

EUGENE. Not in the least, Monsieur; I beg you will not apologise. Consider yourself at home.

CANNEL. You are very polite, Monsieur. Ah! Monsieur Dubois I believe.

EUGENE. Oh! ah! yes—certainly Monsieur Dubois; at your service. (*aside*) I may as well be Dubois, as any one else. It is an excellent travelling name, almost as good as Smith, to which our English neighbours are so partial. (*to* CANNELLE) I am as you say — Monsieur Dubois. Whom have I the pleasure of addressing?

CANNEL. Permit me to introduce myself as Monsieur Cannelle, ex-mayor of Courville.

EUGENE. Ah! Monsieur Cannelle, grocer at the Mandarin and Sugar Loaf.

CANNEL. Grocer if you will; but let me assure you that I have a soul above cinnamon and treacle. Monsieur is travelling, I believe?

EUGENE. Travelling—yes. (*aside*) Very inquisitive!

CANNEL. For pleasure or for business may I ask?

EUGENE. Why, partly for one and the other. It saves an immensity of time.

CANNEL. Is Monsieur travelling in my line?

EUGENE. Not in your line, Monsieur Cannelle; I am amusing myself here before I proceed to Lyons.

CANNEL. What a curious coincidence! I have a cousin at Lyons; perhaps, Monsieur Dubois, you may know him, or you may have heard of him—my cousin, Phillipe Dochefort—a notary.

EUGENE. Dochefort! No, indeed, Monsieur Cannelle—I never had that honour. (*aside*) Tiresome old twaddler, why don't he go? (*to* CANNELLE) So, your cousin lives at Lyons?

CANNEL. Yes; and great a man as he thinks himself now—he was only a poor lad here at Courville, the son of the old steward, Nicole Pataud.

EUGENE. (*eagerly*) Pataud!—Pataud! did you say?

CANNEL. Yes—Pataud—neither more nor less; but he succeeded to a fortune, in some unexpected manner; married a rich wife—and is now the respected notary, Dochefort.

EUGENE. (*aside*) Philippe Pataud—the very man of whom I am in search. (*to* CANNELLE) Monsieur Cannelle, I find your conversation so very pleasing, that I trust you will not think of leaving me just yet. I am going to breakfast; do me the favour of sharing my repast. (*goes*, L. 1 E.) Barbeau! Barbeau! Is breakfast ready? Mind—covers for two. Monsieur Cannelle joins me.

CANNEL. Monsieur, I accept with pleasure. (*aside*) Do

me the favour—I think that to an Ex-mayor, he might have said—do me the honour. One can easily see that he is *not* a man of rank.

Enter BARBEAU, L. 1 E., *with tray, on which are covered dishes, glasses, wine bottles, plates, &c.*

BARB. Here you are, monsieur—the most delicate cutlets, à la Maintenon. (*places tray on table—then brings forward chairs,* R. *and* L.)

EUGENE. (*to* CANNELLE) Be seated, I beg, monsieur. (*they sit—*EUGENE, R., CANNELLE, L.) A glass of wine, Monsieur Cannelle—I can safely recommend Barbeau's wine; especially when he does not, by mistake, draw it out of the vinegar cask. (*pours out wine—they drink, having first touched glasses in the French fashion*)

BARB. Monsieur is pleased to be witty. (*aside*) At my expense, Parbleu! that adds another item to the bill.

EUGENE. (*helps* CANNELLE) Now Monsieur Cannelle, I should like to have your opinion of the cutlet. Barbeau, we shall do very well—you need not wait. (*they eat*)

BARB. I was going to forget a most important piece of information, and that monsieur will be charmed to hear. The owner of the Chateau de Courville is hourly expected!

EUGENE. (*looks up*) Is he? Then I strongly recommend him to set the stonemasons and bricklayers to work.

BARB. And Monsieur Cannelle informs me that he is coming *Incog*—there!

EUGENE. Oh, he comes *Incog*—With all my heart!

BARB. As this hotel is *the* hotel, of course he will do me the honour of coming here.

EUGENE. Well, he might do worse, Barbeau. Monsieur Cannelle, you positively eat nothing.

CANNEL. Thanks, Monsieur, I do very well—in fact I am doing justice to this excellent breakfast.

EUGENE. Another glass of wine to our better acquaintance. (*they drink*)

BARB. But, Monsieur—in case the illustrious traveller should come here——

EUGENE. Meaning the owner of the chateau yonder, I

consider him as a benefactor to all the owls and bats of the province.

BARB. A benefactor—Oh, he will doubtless become one to others, as well as to the bats and owls—But I was about to observe——

EUGENE. As usual!—Barbeau, you are a man of great observation.

BARB. Monsieur is pleased to compliment me. I was about to observe—the gentleman, who may arrive, will require a room.

EUGENE. Of course he will: you are not in the habit of lodging your guests in the pigstye.

BARB. And, as I have but one *best* bed room, that which you occupy—Monsieur——

EUGENE. Put the illustrious traveller into the second-best bed room.

BARB. Oh! monsieur really is joking! The idea of putting my feudal lord, the owner of Courville, into the second-best bed room! Most decidedly, I decline the proposal. In fact, monsieur, I must request that you will be so good as to give up the apartment you occupy.

EUGENE. (*rises—comes forward*) Upon my word, Barbeau, you are the funniest, the most facetious, and the most fussy little fellow I ever had the good fortune to encounter. So you coolly ask me to turn out of my comfortable room, and for a stranger?

BARB. Consider, Monsieur. This, the Seigneur of the village, who may arrive, even to-day.

EUGENE. It would not in the least surprise me if he were to drop in unexpectedly, and perhaps to-day.

CANNEL. (*rises—comes forward*) Does Monsieur Dubois know him? our new proprietor, who has left Paris; and is said to be on his road to Courville.

BARB. Does monsieur know the gentleman?

EUGENE. Well, I believe I do know something about him.

BARB. Does he resemble the late illustrious Marquis, of happy memory?

EUGENE. It is to be hoped not; for the late Marquis was not celebrated for personal beauty. Was he not hump-backed, and rather disposed to squint?

CANNEL. Oh, dear no! Monsieur Dubois. It was merely a slight elevation of the shoulder, and a trifling obliquity of vision.

EUGENE. I can assure you then the present lord of the village is very like other two-legged beings. I am sorry to disappoint your expectations; but he has no hump, and his eyes always look the same way at once. (*sits at table*)

Enter LE DOUX *hastily from door*, R.

LE D. Good morning, gentlemen—Ah—Ouf! (*fans himself with his three-cornered hat*) How terribly I am out of breath! But I ran all the way from the Barrier to tell Barbeau that the illustrious traveller is coming.

BARB. }
CANNEL. } You don't say so!

LE D. 'Tis a fact—He is actually coming!—You must know that I was taking a little stroll just to renovate my ideas touching the composition of a masterpiece of confectionary, on which I am engaged, when, what should I see coming down the hill, but a caleche and four, at full gallop. I regret to say, that within a few yards of the foot, the leaders fell, and over went the carriage, into a ditch, which, very fortunately, happened to be a dry one. My dear friends, I do assure you, that, at that moment, I was shaking all over—like one of my own cream custards. Imagine what we should have felt, had the Marquis been in the mud.

BARB. Horrible—too horrible to think of—but go on, Le Doux.

LE D. When I had sufficiently recovered from the shock, I advanced, and making three distinct bows—you know I am renowned for the grace of my bows——

BARB. Oh, bother your bows—do tell us what happened next.

LE D. Friend Barbeau—you are mighty impatient! Well, having bowed, I helped his lordship out of the ditch, and on being questioned as to where he could go to refresh himself, I told him that he could not do better than put up at the "Golden Goose." So while the postillions busied themselves in raising the carriage and horses, I ran on to apprize you.

BARB. (*to* EUGENE) Oh, Monsieur Dubois—do you hear that?

EUGENE. (*still seated*) Yes; it must have been very amusing to every one but the principal performer.

BARB. But surely you will not refuse to give up your apartment—you hear that the Marquis has been upset.

EUGENE. (*rises—comes forward*) So much the better for the coachmaker—there will be a job for him.

CANNEL. But Monsieur the Marquis has been thrown into a ditch! and most likely is injured.

EUGENE. So much the better for the doctor—there will be a patient for him.

BARB. But, Monsieur, do consider——

EUGENE. Barbeau—don't bother! Here I am; and I promise you that while the seigneur of the village is here, here I also shall and will remain. Why, where on earth, man, would you have me go?

CANNEL. Oh, Monsieur Dubois, I shall be happy to receive you: Madame Cannelle will be enchanted at making your acquaintance; you will find her the model of domestic virtues. I need only observe, that her café à la creme is faultless. Then, Monsieur—our daughter——

EUGENE. Oh, ho! you have a daughter, Monsieur Cannelle.

CANNEL. A charming girl of seventeen—Mademoiselle Juliette Adolphine, one of the best matches in the country —beautiful—accomplished.

LE D. I have the honour of being her godfather, Monsieur, and I can vouch for the truth of the assertion. You should see her drawings—a head of Scipio Africanus —that would do credit, even to the Louvre.

EUGENE. My good Monsieur Le Doux, I don't understand drawing.

CANNELLE. And then, Monsieur Dubois, if you admire family portraits, we have in our saloon, I may say, a rare collection: first, the likenesses of Madame Cannelle and of your humble servant, represented as a shepherdess and shepherd of Arcadia; but the *gem* of our treasures of art, is the portrait of Mademoiselle de Courville, the sister of the late Marquis, to whom Madame Cannelle had the honour of being femme de chambre.

EUGENE. (*eagerly*) How! Madame Cannelle knew Madame—I mean Mademoiselle de Courville?

CANNEL. Most intimately: she was brought up with her from childhood, and only left her when she married me. Ah, Monsieur Dubois, that picture alone would tempt an amateur—My cousin, Phillipe Dochefort, would give anything to possess it.

EUGENE. Say no more, Monsieur Cannelle—I accept your obliging offer. The portraits, and, above all, the head of Scipio Africanus, have decided me. I shall be happy to become an inmate of your house—(*aside*) I shall learn now something of this Dochefort, who has hitherto been such a mystery to me. (*to* BARBEAU) Now, Barbeau, my little bill—quick!

BARB. Your little bill, Monsieur Dubois—here it is, just fifteen francs. (*presents bill*)

EUGENE. And very reasonable, too: here is a louis—give the change to my friend Picard—let him drink to the health of the new proprietor, and strongly recommend him at the same time to polish the gentleman's boots a little better than he has mine. Now, Monsieur Cannelle, in two seconds I am at your service. *Exit door*, L. 3 E.

BARB. Monsieur Cannelle, you *are* in luck; I know that Monsieur Dubois must be rich; he pays like a prince —and, then he is unmarried—you have a daughter—who knows what may not happen.

Re-enter EUGENE, *door*, L. 3 E.

EUGENE. Monsieur Cannelle, I am ready—Barbeau, let my portmanteau be sent after me. (*smacking of whip without*) What is all that noise about?

Enter PICARD, *door*, R.

PICARD. Oh, master! master!—here's the great gentle-man—He's a coming—he's at the door!

BARB. I fly to receive him. Get along—do, stupid!
(*pushes* PICARD *out before him, door*, R.—CANNELLE *and* LE DOUX *run and look out at window*)

EUGENE. So the new seigneur du village is here at last; I must, unknown to him, catch a glimpse of this very august personage, for whom I am so unceremoniously dismissed. (*opens door*, R.) Here he comes—Ah!—surely I know him—yes; it is the same—Ha, ha, ha! this is an excellent joke, and one by which I hope to profit: No one will recognise me. (*slouches his hat over his eyes—pulls up his coat collar*) In case I am scrutinised, this will sufficiently conceal my features. Now Monsieur, the Ex-mayor, I am at your service.

CANNEL. (*comes forward*, L.) In a moment; I only await the entrance of the illustrious personage—he comes.

The door, R., is suddenly flung open. Enter BARBEAU and PICARD bowing in, and preceding MARCEL, who swaggers in—he should be very gaudily dressed in the Louis Quinze style—powdered hair—three-cornered hat, bordered with gold lace, with brilliant loop—velvet coat —satin waistcoat—shoes, with red heels, and paste buckles—and sword, which is perpetually getting between his legs—EUGENE stands aside as he enters, and slips out unperceived at door, R.

BARB. (*bowing very low*) Welcome, Monseigneur—I mean Monsieur, welcome to the "Golden Goose."

PICARD. (*awkwardly imitating him*) Yes; welcome, monsieur—monseigneur I mean, welcome to the "Golden Goose."

BARB. (*pulling PICARD by the ear*) Booby—*will* you be quiet, and go away. (*pushes PICARD out door*, R.)

MARCEL. (C., *affectedly looking round*) So this is the "Golden Goose?" You, I presume, are the landlord—. A chair. (BARBEAU *brings a chair from table—*MARCEL *sits*) Another for my feet. (BARBEAU *brings forward second chair, on which* MARCEL *puts up his legs*)

CANNEL. (*to* LE DOUX) Evidently a great man—(*advances*) Monsieur, I trust, is not seriously injured.

MARCEL. (*looks at* CANNELLE) Landlord!—Who is that fellow?

BARB. Oh, Monseigneur—Monsieur, I mean; with all deference, that gentleman is not a fellow—he is a Monsieur Cannelle.

CANNEL. Ex-mayor of the town—at the service of

Monsieur. I have long been honoured with the custom of the late Marquis.

MARCEL. (*starts up*) Monsieur Cannelle, did you say? Excellent Monsieur Cannelle, I have the honour of making the acquaintance of the ex-mayor. (*aside*) Confound him—I must be civil. He is the father of my adorable Adolphine. (*to* CANNELLE) I really have the pleasure of addressing the ex-mayor of——

CANNEL. Of Courville, Monsieur. (*bows very low*)

MARCEL. So this delicious abode is *the* Courville of which I have heard so much. (*aside*) Oh, blind goddess Fortune, why did you let me be upset into a dry ditch in this place?—I should have preferred the dirtiest of horse-ponds, in any other locality. (*to* CANNELLE) Your friend there, is, if I mistake not, the kind person who extricated me from my unpleasant position, in the ditch yonder.

LE D. (*bows*) The same, Monseigneur—I mean, Monsieur—My name is Le Doux, confectioner en chef to the late Marquis, and also, I may add, to the nobility and gentry of the province.

MARCEL. Really, you are Monseiur Le Doux, whose delicate productions have immortalised his name. (*aside*) Hang it! he is my stepmother's brother: I have fallen among foes!

LE D. I flatter myself, that when monsieur has tasted my last great achievement, he will be convinced that I am worthy of the good opinion he has of my poor talent.

MARCEL. Oh, Monsieur Le Doux, I have had an opportunity of tasting some of your excellent pastry; (*aside*) and of suffering fearful indigestions in consequence. But, gentlemen, I fear that I am detaining you.

CANNEL. ⎫
LE D. ⎬ Oh, not in the least, Monsieur.

MARCEL. And I must now retire to my apartment. Here, landlord!

BARB. Barbeau, of the "Golden Goose," at the service of monseigneur—I mean, of monsieur!

MARCEL. These gentlemen will dine with me, I hope; meantime, Monsieur Cannelle and Monsieur Le Doux will excuse my taking leave of them, now—I have letters of importance to write.

CANNEL. We will no longer intrude on monsieur.

LE D. We respectfully take our leave of monsieur.

MARCEL. Au revoir, gentlemen—we dine at four precisely—Barbeau, mind, we shall expect a first-rate dinner—everything of the best.

CANNEL. (bows) Au revoir, monsieur!

> *Exeunt* CANNELLE *and* LE DOUX, *door* R., *after many bows, as if each wished to give the precedence to the other, finally* CANNELLE *goes out first, with great dignity, followed by* LE DOUX.

BARB. Monsieur has no other commands to give.

MARCEL. None. By-the-bye, my hair is a little disordered—have you a hairdresser, or a decent barber in the place?—if so, send him to me.

BARB. We have an excellent perruquieur, who will be charmed to wait on monsieur.

MARCEL. Good. Now leave me.

BARB. (bows) I obey. (aside) One can see, with half an eye, that he must be a very great man indeed.

> *Exit door*, L. 1 E.

MARCEL. (throws himself into a chair) Ha, ha, ha!—I shall expire with laughing. What wonderful politeness! I am evidently mistaken for a great man, travelling incog—but who I am supposed to be, is a perfect mystery to me. I would rather have arrived at any other town, however " vogue la galère." I shall be for the nonce, whoever they please—count, duke, or even a prince of the blood!

> *Enter* EUGENE, *cautiously, from door* R. 1 E.; *he goes behind* MARCEL; *taps him on the shoulder.*

MARCEL. (looking up) What is it, friend?

EUGENE. A word with you, monsieur.

MARCEL. A word with me! Really, I have not the honour of your acquaintance.

EUGENE. Possibly not. Yet, if I remember rightly—and my memory is pretty correct—you are one Marcel, clerk to Monsieur Nicholas Vichy, notary of Paris.

MARCEL. (starting up) Sir—you are——

EUGENE. No, but *you* are; travelling on private business, relating to a client of Monsieur Vichy's. You are, or ought to be, on the road to Lyons; but your carriage breaks down here, and you very naturally take refuge in the first inn you come to.

MARCEL. That is not high treason, I should imagine.

EUGENE. Certainly not; but some people might object to your opening a valise of which you had the key, and putting on a coat, waistcoat, and sword, to which you are not entitled—eh, Master Marcel?

MARCEL. (*aside*) How could he find that out? (*to* EUGENE) I protest, sir, that I do not comprehend you.

EUGENE. I speak pretty plainly, I think; and I must own that you do not look at all amiss in your borrowed plumes. (*walks round* MARCEL)

MARCEL. In the name of wonder who are you? You seem intimately acquainted with me.

EUGENE. Monsieur Cannelle, the grocer and ex-mayor, who did me the favour of breakfasting with me this morning, and who is to have the honour of dining with you this afternoon, at the expense of your master's client—he will tell you that I am named Dubois.

MARCEL. Dubois!—Dubois!—a very general name! Well, Monsieur Dubois, what do you require of me?

EUGENE. That you will on no account undeceive these good people here, who have mistaken you for a gentleman of rather higher rank than you are. Continue to personate him; and contrive to extract from Cannelle all the intelligence you can respecting the sister of the late marquis. You will oblige me, and I shall not be ungrateful. *Exit,* R. *door.*

MARCEL. Who can that mysterious individual be? I must serve him, or he may betray me to Cannelle—and then, farewell all my hopes of obtaining the hand of Juliette Adolphine.

Enter LE DOUX *cautiously, door* L. 1 E.

LE D. Hist—hist, monsieur——

MARCEL. Ah, Monsieur Le Doux. (*aside*) What can he want?

B

LE D. (*mysteriously*) Might I be so bold as to intrude on monsieur's precious time.

MARCEL. Most certainly, Monsieur Le Doux; in what way can I serve you?

LE D. Monsieur is too good; I fear that I am very presuming, but my object is to be of use to monseigneur —I mean monsieur.

MARCEL. Ah, indeed! and in what way?

LE D. Monsieur has certainly a right to appear here Incog, and we should respect the scruples of a great man.

MARCEL. My good Monsieur Le Doux, why *will* you insist on mistaking me for a great man—I am merely a plain, unpretending traveller.

LE D. Just as monsieur pleases. But I know that you are interested in the affairs of the family of Courville.

MARCEL. The Courvilles! Ah, let me see—did they not formerly reside at the old chateau here?

LE D. The late marquis did till the death of his sister, who was many years his junior. Ah, monsieur, I could tell you terrible tales of the old chateau.

MARCEL. I suppose that it has a respectable assortment of family ghosts and hereditary hobgoblins!

LE D. Oh! worse than that. You must know that, many years ago, there was a beautiful young lady at the chateau:

MARCEL. I am sorry that it was many years ago, because time is very damaging to beauty. Pray who was this beautiful young lady?

LE D. Sister to the marquis! And there is the mystery!

MARCEL. I confess that I see nothing very mysterious in that circumstance, because *I* happen to have a sister. Is that all the information? (*aside*) Shall I be able to extract any intelligence from this compound of puff-paste and sugar!

LE D. But this sister, monsieur, disappeared in a very mysterious manner.

MARCEL. Oh, ho!—it was the manner, not the lady which constituted the mystery. So she disappeared?

LE D. And has never been heard of since. Now as the late Marquis died unmarried, this lady, if living, is the next heir.

MARCEL. Precisely so.

Le D. And as no one ever heard of her again, she must be dead; and the greater part of the estates must go to a stranger, formerly the son of the old steward.

Marcel. Yes, I see. You mean—monsieur—monsieur—dear me, how stupid of me to forget a name—(*aside*) which I never remember to have heard.

Le D. Monsieur Dochefort—formerly a Pataud—now a notary at Lyons.

Marcel. Dochefort—of Lyons, did you say?

Le D. Dochefort—and he it was who gave us a hint that monseignenr—monsieur I mean—might be travelling this way.

Marcel. Did he? (*aside*) So, my old master, Dochefort, has a finger in this. He has never forgiven me for running away from him and his rogueries. A pleasant circle of unwelcome acquaintance I have tumbled into. (*to* Le Doux) But with respect to this Dochefort?

Le D. We all suspect, here, that he knew what became of Mademoiselle de Courville, and that she was— (Can- nelle *is seen passing the window*) Dear me, here comes that tedious fellow, Cannelle. I don't want him to see me with monsieur—he would suspect that I suspected something. Au revoir, monsieur. I shall have the pleasure of renewing this conversation at a more convenient time. Beware of Cannelle—he and Dochefort are cousins, and hand and glove, as one may say. He will be wanting——

Marcel. To pump me, you would say?

Le D. Monsieur has just hit upon the truth. I must not be seen here—I shall return when there is no fear of interruption. (*aside*) What a wonderful family likeness! he is every inch a Courville. *Exit, door* l. 1 e.

Marcel. Well, my Incog is doing some good to the other gentleman, who is also Incog. I wonder who he is!—and I should like to know who I am supposed to be! Mum—here comes my intended father-in-law.

Enter Cannelle, *cautiously, door*, r.

Marcel. Ah! Monsieur Cannelle, this is indeed kind of you.

Cannel. Oh! monsieur, could I speak two words to you?

MARCEL. Two hundred, if you will, excellent Monsieur Cannelle. If our conference is to be a long one, we had better be seated. (*brings forward a chair—*CANNELLE *does the same—they sit*) And now I am all attention, monsieur.

CANNEL. Monsieur will not deem me impertinent if I venture to say that I know he is deeply interested in the affairs of the family of Courville.

MARCEL. Well—a little—yes, I am rather so; you understand, Monsieur Cannelle—a word to the wise——

CANNEL. And you are perhaps aware that there has been something wrong there?

MARCEL. Yes—a screw loose somewhere, and an immensity of botheration.

CANNEL. There is, monsieur—and a relative of mine is unfortunately mixed up with it.

MARCEL. Really—vastly unpleasant that; but what has the botheration to do with me?

CANNEL. Monsieur, I could tell you a secret about that family, which may affect the present heir.

MARCEL. Oh, oh, a secret!—out with it then—who is it about?

CANNEL. The sister—Mademoiselle de Courville—who disappeared;—yes, Mademoiselle Adolphine.

MARCEL. Adolphine, did you say!—what a charming name! Do you know, Monsieur Cannelle, that I quite adore the name of Adolphine, and I would choose a wife of that name, above all others.

CANNEL. How very remarkable that my daughter—my only child—should be named Adolphine.

MARCEL. Very remarkable!—She is a mere child, I suppose?

CANNEL. Oh, no, monsieur—not a child—an accomplished young lady of eighteen, whose education was completed at Paris—But to my story——

MARCEL. (*interrupting him*) Sweet Adolphine!—That name will run in my head all day, and I shall dream of it all night. Of course, your daughter is surrounded by adorers?

CANNEL. Well, sir, she might choose from among the most eligible matches in the province; but to the business in question, monsieur, touching this sister of the late marquis, who is—Allow me first to ascertain if no one can overhear us.

Goes cautiously to door, L. 1 E., *opens it, and* BARBEAU *enters suddenly.*

Good gracious, Barbeau! what brings you here? (*aside*) If he has listened.

BARB. (*to* MARCEL) I have the honour of announcing to monsieur, that the hairdresser awaits his pleasure.

MARCEL. Only the hairdresser: let him come in.
Exit BARBEAU, *door* L.

CANNEL. As we are interrupted, monsieur, I take my leave for the present; but allow me to continue this conversation when you are more at leisure.

MARCEL. I shall be enchanted. *Exit* CANNELLE, *door* R. Fortunately, neither old Le Doux nor Cannelle can recognise me. It is seven years since either of them saw me. What would the latter say, if he learnt that *I* am the secret adorer of the lovely Adolphine, whom I saw at Paris—and whom I mean to marry? Oh, why am I only clerk to a notary!

Enter BARBEAU, *door* L., *speaking as he enters.*

BARB. Yes; you can come in, Monsieur Le Blanc.

MARCEL. (*starts*) Eh?—whom did you say?

BARB. Monsieur le Blanc, the hair-dresser. Oh! quite a paragon, I assure you. He comes from Paris; and wields his powder-puff better than any man in the province. *Exit* BARBEAU, *door* L. 1 E.

MARCEL. Oh, my prophetic soul!—it is uncle Peter Achilles—who believes me to be scribbling at this present moment, in the office of Monsieur Vichy, at Paris. How shall I be able to impose upon him? Here he comes, to exercise his art upon my head—he has often exercised his cane upon my shoulders. Should he presume to recognise me! I must brazen it out that I am not myself. (MARCEL *sits with his back towards door,* L., *takes out a letter, pretends to read*) I can amuse myself with my tailor's bill.

(*during this Scene,* LE BLANC *should be constantly endeavouring to obtain a glimpse of* MARCEL's *face, which* MARCEL *prevents, by either turning his*

*back to him, or else by holding the powdering mask
before his face—*MARCEL *also speaks in a feigned
voice)*

Enter LE BLANC *as a hair-dresser of the time,* L.; *he
carries a dressing gown over his arm, and has in one
hand a powder mask and a dressing case.*

LE BLANC. I have the honour to pay my respects to
monsieur——

MARCEL. (*in rather a gruff voice*) Monsieur le Blanc,
I believe? I suppose that you can dress a gentleman's
hair?

LE BLANC. I dressed the late Marquis de Courville's
scores and scores of times. (*pulls out his comb, powder-
box, &c.*) Will monsieur permit me to divest him of his
coat, and to assist him in putting on this powdering robe
de chambre.

MARCEL. There, never mind my coat; just throw the
gown over my shoulders. (*rises, stands with his back to*
LE BLANC *who places the gown on him*) Now for the
mask. (*snatches powder mask from* LE BLANC *and holds
it before his face)* And now, make haste.

LE BLANC. Monsieur shall look like an Adonis, with
the mere application of my comb and powder-puff. (*begins
dressing* MARCEL'S *hair*) Monsieur has just arrived from
Paris, I believe?

MARCEL. (*gruffly*) Yes, you know Paris?

LE BLANC. I formerly resided in it—and I have still
a wild scamp of a nephew there.

MARCEL. Indeed! Does he follow your trade?

LE BLANC. My art, you mean, monsieur? No, he dis-
dains it; he is clerk to a notary—one Monsieur Vichy—
he is the son of my only sister, by name, Jules Marcel.
I should have made him my heir, but now, with monseigneur's permission, I mean to marry.

MARCEL. My good Le Blanc, are you not rather too
old to think of marrying. (*aside*) If uncle Peter marries,
good-bye to my inheritance.

LE BLANC. Oh, no, monsieur, the young lady's friends
are willing enough—they will give their consent.

MARCEL. (*aside*) Very pleasant news! (*to* LE BLANC) But the young lady herself may object——

LE BLANC. Oh, monsieur, I flatter myself that she will not object. My magazine will receive a charming mistress, whose accomplishments are first rate. You should hear her play and sing—you should see her drawings, and in particular, a head of Scipio Africanus, from the antique. I tell her it would be perfection if it had been represented in a perriwig; though Monsieur Cannelle assures me it is classically correct.

MARCEL. (*eagerly*) What name did you say?

LE BLANC. Cannelle, our worthy ex-mayor, whose daughter I shall have the honour of making my wife.

MARCEL. (*starts up, throws the powder-box, puff, and powder mask at* LE BLANC, *who is seized with a violent fit of sneezing*) What—you—you presuming old powder-puff —you marry grace, youth, and beauty? Go to the—the —the Antipodes! (*throws the dressing gown over* LE BLANC) Oh, Adolphine! Adolphine!

> *Exit, door* L. 3 E.—*presently, a violent ringing of bells is heard.*

LE BLANC. Good gracious! what can all this mean? I begin to think that the illustrious traveller must be mad. What has my marriage to do with him?

Enter BARBEAU, *door* L. 1 E.

BARB. I say, neighbour Le Blanc, what have you said or done to the illustrious gentleman?

LE BLANC. Done!—Nothing at all! His lordship was chatting with me in a most charming familiar manner, when all at once he jumps up in a fury, throws the robe de chambre over me, almost blinds me with a perfect avalanche of powder, thumps his own illustrious forehead, and then rushes out of the room like a maniac!

BARB. You have offended his dignity, Le Blanc, and have brought eternal disgrace on the " Golden Goose !"

LE BLANC. Barbeau, you are an old fool! Offend his dignity, indeed! Never presume to send for me to dress the calves' heads of your customers! (*gathers up the things* MARCEL *threw at him, and amongst them the letter*

Marcel *was reading*) Good morning, Barbeau. I wish you better luck with the next illustrious person who is travelling incog. *Exit angrily, door* R.

Barb. What can he have said to my guest? I must find out; and here is a packet of letters for him from old Cannelle. (*bell rings*) Coming, monsieur.

Exit, door L. 3 E.

Enter Eugene, *door* R.

Eugene. I have watched them all out—the last departure from the levee of the great man being the little hairdresser! who appeared terribly discomposed. I trust that he has no suspicions respecting Marcel, for on that young clerk rests my hopes of obtaining the information I require. Not a word can I learn from Madame Cannelle, Heavens! every hour that detains me here gives this Dochefort time to put his wicked plans into execution.

Enter Barbeau, *door* L. 3 E.

Barb. (*speaking as he enters*) Yes, monsieur, I will attend to it directly. Ah! young gentleman, (*to* Eugene) you are the very person that is wanted. The illustrious traveller, who for the present chooses to remain Incog, does you the honour of wishing to see you immediately in his private apartment. Now pray make haste—great men must not be kept waiting.

Eugene. Decidedly not, Barbeau—I shall go to him.

Exit, door L. 3 E.

Barb. That young man doesn't seem to know his place in society: with what familiarity he speaks of monseigneur. Now I must prepare the table for dinner. Here, Picard, Picard, bring a clean cloth—help me to place the knives and forks.

Enter Picard, *with a cloth and tray, door* L. 1 E.

Picard. Here you are, master—all ready!

Barb. There, there, make haste, and tell cook to hurry the dinner.

Picard. The cook!—you mean mistress: you had better tell her yourself, master—I don't want to have my head broken any more with the rolling pin.

BARB. Picard, you are a terrible dolt—get away with you, do.

PICARD. Ah! master knows the weight of that rolling pin as well as I do. *Exit, door*, L. 1 E.

BARB. (*arranging the table*) Now, where ought the great man to sit?—At the head of the table, of course. Cannelle, as ex-mayor, on his right—Le Doux on his left —though I expect they will quarrel for the best place. Why I declare, here they come, and disputing about something.

Enter CANNELLE *and* LE DOUX, *from door*, R.

CANNEL. (*speaking as he enters*) Are you really quite certain, Le Doux?

LE D. Oh, quite positive; the messenger arrived on horseback; he told the mayor that he was the bearer of a most important letter for a gentleman who had been staying here for some time. The mayor referred him here, and the man hurried away before I could even catch a glimpse of the letter.—Is not that very mysterious?

CANNEL. Bless me! what can it mean? I have it— the two great men are both here Incog.

BARB. (*advancing*, L.) *The* two!—which two?

CANNEL. The two heirs—the cousin who has just arrived, and—— (*aside*) I was nearly letting the secret out.

BARB. Another heir!—impossible! Oh, there can be but one—*the* illustrious gentleman who came in his carriage, and who must be monseigneur; besides, re-member the wonderful family likeness that you discovered immediately, Monsieur Cannelle.

CANNEL. True; the very eyes of the late Marquis, save that he does not squint.

LE D. And the figure the very counterpart as well— only——

BARB. The young gentleman has no hump. Should he happen not to be the right one! Suppose that I have turned the real heir out of his room to make way for the false one!

CANNEL. Nonsense, Barbeau. He must be the real

heir—I mean the gentleman who has invited us to dinner.

Enter LE BLANC *hurriedly, door* R.

Why, neighbour Le Blanc, what a flurry you are in!

LE BLANC. Flurry, indeed! well I may be in a flurry! I have made such a discovery!

CANNEL. }
LE D. } A discovery! What is it?

LE BLANC. You know that I was sent for to dress the hair of a gentleman who is here incog?

BARB. Yes, yes—we know that—go on!

LE BLANC. Well, although I dressed his hair in the first style, and chatted to him in the most agreeable manner, he suddenly took offence at something I said, bounced out of his chair, flung at me everything he could lay his hands on, and then darted out of the room. Well, in gathering my things together, I picked up a note—a most mysterious note——

CANNEL. Which you read?

LE BLANC. Which I read; and guess my surprise when I found that it was neither more nor less than a tailor's bill—for repairing and turning a coat. Did one ever hear of such a thing as a great man and a nobleman turning his coat?

CANNEL. I am compelled to say that I have. But to the discovery, Le Blanc.

LE BLANC. The discovery! Why, that I think the traveller is no more a great man than I am?

CANNEL. Nonsense, man! Did you observe his features —he has the family nose to perfection!

LE BLANC. I can answer for it, that he has the family temper to a fault. But the gentleman contrived to keep his face turned from me the whole time I was powdering his hair—I couldn't judge of the likeness.

LE D. A thought strikes me! Barbeau, have you not a young man staying here?

BARB. Yes; perhaps the paper belongs to him—the great man number one has sent for him, and they are now together in the best bed room. Hush! I thought that I heard loud talking. (*listens at door*, L. 3 E.)

CANNELLE. Surely they are not going to quarrel, and perhaps have a duel; for in that case *I* as ex-mayor must really interfere.

LE D. Had I not better run and apprise our friend the doctor that he may be wanted; the wounded gentleman will require all our care.

LE BLANC. Had you not better wait till he *is* wounded?

LE D. He will not be able to remain here, the inn would be far too noisy. I can offer the unfortunate gentleman a superb apartment, and every attention.

BARB. Mind your own business, Monsieur le Doux; attend to your own pie crusts and patties, and leave me to look after my own customers.

CANNEL. Hush, hush! my good friends, for goodness sake don't let us quarrel! Who knows that perhaps the two illustrious gentlemen may, at this very moment, be giving each other a deadly wound. I am going to reconnoitre.

LE BLANC. Reconnoitre? bless me! how shall you manage that?

CANNEL. Through the keyhole. (*goes cautiously towards door* L. 3 E., *followed on tiptoe by* LE DOUX *and* LE BLANC) They have put the key in the inside; I can see nothing, but I can listen. Hush! what is that?

BARB. What is it?

CANNEL. Nothing! all is quiet. Oh, if there were but a crevice through which one could peep.

(*as all are trying to peep through the keyhole the door is suddenly opened, and* MARCEL *enters, in a plain travelling dress—*LE DOUX, LE BLANC, *and* CANNELLE *are thrown down*)

MARCEL. Monsieur Cannelle, a million of pardons!

CANNEL. (*scrambles up, the others rise*) Oh, Monseigneur, there is no need to apologise.

MARCEL. Barbeau, you must get the carriage ready instantly; we start in half an hour. Let me have your bill.

BARB. Start in half an hour! But the dinner that monsieur has commanded? and which will be superb——

MARCEL. These gentlemen will eat it, and I pay for it; only *do* hurry the Postillions—we must reach Lyons to-

night. Now be quick. (*pushes* Barbeau *out at door*, L. 1 E.)
What a fortunate discovery for us! Gentlemen, I hope
to meet you again, but——

Cannel. *and* Le D. Oh, monseigneur—that is monsieur.

Le Blanc. (*advances*, c.) Monseigneur (*looks at* Marcel
and then staggers back, R.) Can I believe my eyes! His
very look; his very voice.

Marcel. What is the matter with the little barber?
(*walks away—aside*) Uncle Peter is astonished rather.

Cannel. (*to* Le Blanc) What you also are struck with
the wonderful likeness to the late marquis.

Le Blanc. (*angrily*) The late marquis! late fiddlesticks!
If I am Peter Achilles Le Blanc, that must be——

Le D. Monseigneur—I said so, did I not?

Marcel. My good friends, how often have I told you
that I am merely a plain traveller? I am no monseigneur
at all.

Le Blanc. No indeed! I can vouch for the truth of
that, for as I am an honest man——

Cannel. My dear friend, be cautious, pray do.

Le Blanc. As I live then, monseigneur, as you *will*
style him, is no other than my scape-grace of a nephew.

Cannel. (*to* Le Doux) Your nephew? Impossible!

Le Blanc. My nephew I tell you—Jules Marcel: let
him deny it if he can.

Marcel. Gentlemen, I really am Jules Marcel, clerk
to Monsieur Vichy, notary of Paris.

Le D. Jules Marcel! the step-son of my sister!

Cannel. Jules Marcel, the good-for-nothing scamp,
who has presumed to fall in love with my daughter.

Marcel. Gently, gently, papa Cannelle; if loving your
daughter, the charming Adolphine, be a crime, there is old
uncle Peter as great a culprit as myself. Now go and
abuse him.

Le Blanc. So *you* are the formidable rival whom
Mademoiselle Cannelle prefers?

Marcel. I am; and I applaud her good taste—why,
uncle Peter, you wouldn't have her marry her grandfather.

Cannel. (*in a rage*) That *I*—Cannelle—ex-mayor,
should have been so duped—so deceived! Why I have
been as respectful to him!—How dared you allow me to

continue in error, you low-born fellow, and mistake you for the marquis?

LE BLANC. Low-born fellow! my nephew is every bit as well born as yourself, neighbour Cannelle. I should like to know what has become of the wonderful family likeness you both discovered, and were so angry with me for not seeing with half an eye?

LE D. If you are not the heir of Courville, I should like to know who is?

MARCEL. I shall be delighted to introduce him. (*opens door,* L. 3 E.)

Enter EUGENE, *dressed as a nobleman of the time,* L. 3 E.

Allow me to present to the real heir of Courville, some of his most humble servants. Ha! ha! ha! (*nudges* CANNELLE) Come, papa Cannelle, ex-mayor, can't you make a pretty little speech on the occasion?

CANNEL. That gentleman the heir? why he is——

EUGENE. Eugene Paul de Roseville, nephew of the late marquis, and only son of Eugenie de Courville his sister; whom *you*, Monsieur Cannelle, and your cousin Phillipe Pataud Dochefort, have for years secluded in a convent, pretending that *I*, her son had died in infancy. Here I have the proofs of my birth, the confession of Dochefort, the name of the convent in which my dear mother is, I may say, imprisoned. I stand here the undoubted heir of Courville; Marcel, I shall not forget your zeal; Monsieur Vichy could not have sent me a more clever aide-de-camp. What is the matter, Monsieur the ex-Mayor, you look very crestfallen?

CANNEL. Monseigneur, how can you ever pardon me?

EUGENE. On one condition I will, for I consider you to have been merely the tool of Dochefort, and the past shall be forgotten—provided you give your pretty little daughter to my friend, Jules Marcel, here.

CANNEL. Since monseigneur commands it, of course I consent; but I had partly promised Monsieur Le Blanc.

LE BLANC. Oh! my good friend, since monseigneur is the patron of Jules, I yield my claim; and I have a snug sum laid by to start the young couple in life.

LE D. And I promise not to forget my god-daughter.

MARCEL. Thanks, all; and *I* in turn promise to give you all no reason to repent your kindness. It was rather flattering though to find myself mistaken for a great man travelling incog.

EUGENE. I fear, Marcel, that it was derived chiefly from your borrowed plumes.

MARCEL. Monseigneur, I was only proving the truth of a very homely proverb—" FINE FEATHERS MAKE FINE BIRDS."

| LE B. | CANNEL. | MARCEL. | EUGENE. | LE D. | BARB. |
| R. | | C. | | | L. |

Curtain.

STAGE DIRECTIONS.

| R. | R. C. | C. | L. C. | L. |
| Right | Right Centre. | Centre. | Left Centre. | Left. |

FACING THE AUDIENCE.

THE

POOR RELATION;

OR,

"LOVE ME—LOVE MY DOG!"

A Comic Drama,

IN TWO PARTS.

FOR MALE CHARACTERS ONLY.

THOMAS HAILES LACY,

89, STRAND,

(*Opposite Southampton Street, Covent Garden Market,*)

LONDON.

Characters.

MR. DOWNRIGHT (*a retired Merchant*) ......

JOB DOWNRIGHT ...

HARRY DOWNRIGHT } (*Cousins to Mr. Downright, and now Partners*)

DAVID DOWNRIGHT

TOMPKINS (*Ex-Clerk to Mr. Downright*) ......

WILLIAM LACKWIT (*a Poor Relation*) ......

ROBERT (*Servant to Mr. Downright*) ....

Scene.—A Room in Mr. Downright's House.

Costumes.—MODERN,

Suited to the station and character of the person represented.

THE
POOR RELATION.

PART THE FIRST.

SCENE.—*A Room in Mr. Downright's House; table, c.; chairs, &c.*

Enter DOWNRIGHT *and* TOMPKINS, L.

TOMP. Your resolution is very sudden, Mr. Downright. Are you really bent on leaving England?

DOWN. This very day, Tompkins; and I have sent for you, as one of my most faithful friends, in order that you may be present as a witness, on my part, to an agreement, which I am about to make with my cousins.

TOMP. The three gentlemen to whom you have behaved so generously; and for whose sake you have given up a flourishing business. Why, the firm of Downright has been established for upwards of eighty years.

DOWN. I have realised a competence—I am an old bachelor; and is it not very natural that I should wish to pass the remainder of my days in peace? Why need I toil any more? It is better to let my cousins try their good luck; and I hope they may be as fortunate as myself.

TOMP. Of course, Mr. Downright; it is very good, and very noble of you to provide so handsomely for your relations; but——

DOWN. Oh, my good Tompkins! there is always a *but* in your observations on my three cousins; now, what have you to say against them?

TOMP. Oh, nothing, sir—positively nothing; but——

DOWN. *But*, you are very suspicious.

TOMP. I am very cautious! Do you think it is quite prudent of you to give up everything to your cousins, unconditionally?

A 2

Down. I am sure they will respect my wishes, and carry out my plans. I own that I sometimes have misgivings on the subject of my cautious cousin Job.

Tomp. A regular Job's comforter! He *is* a bird of ill omen—something like Mother Carey's chickens—the certain forerunner of foul weather in the family. He is like a bad barometer—always pointing to stormy. Now, I do allow some good qualities to Mr. David and Mr. Harry—they, at least, are generous. I think, that, in spite of my suspicions, you may trust them a little.

Down. That remains to be proved. I hope I shall not be disappointed in my opinion of them. (*a knock without,* L.) Ah—here they come!—punctual!—that is well!

Tomp. Punctuality is scarcely a virtue, sir, where our interests are so strictly concerned.

Enter ROBERT, L.

Robert. Mr. Harry Downright.

Tomp. (*aside,* R.) Mr. Harry—number one. All fair words, and flummery.

Exit ROBERT, L.

Enter HARRY DOWNRIGHT, L.

Down. I am very happy to see you, cousin Harry.

Harry. (*shakes hands with* Downright) My dear fellow—well—here I am! the first to arrive.

Tomp. (*aside*) His dear fellow! the familiar young puppy: I wonder that he doesn't slap my respected late employer on the back.

Down. Where have you left your two partners? I hope they will not be very much behind-hand.

Harry. My brother David had promised to see a poor fellow, whom we intend to employ—he will be here in a few minutes. As to cousin Job, I left him lecturing the clerks on their shameful waste of ink and wafers in the counting house.

Tomp. Does Mr. Job imagine that the firm of Downright cannot afford to pay a stationer's bill?

Harry. Tompkins—I believe, that if cousin Job had his way, he would compel us to omit the dots to the *i*, and the cross to the *t*; and, in default of wax and wafers, would secure his letters with odd pieces of packthread. Ha, ha, ha!—just like cousin Job!

Tomp. I confess that I do not see the wit of that remark.

Harry. Tompkins, I never suspected you of seeing even as far as the length of your respectable nose. (*a knock*, L.) Here comes the two lags behind.

Enter Robert, L., *shewing in* David, *and* Job Downright.

Robert. Mr. David Downright, Mr. Job Downright.

Down. Good morning, cousins: I am glad to see you. Robert place some chairs at the table. (Robert *places chairs, and exit*, L.) I feel much obliged to you for coming, my kind friends, I will not detain you long, for in an hour I must be on board the steamer.

David. My dear cousin, the pleasure of seeing you is embittered by the knowledge that we shall so soon lose your agreeable society.

Job. (*bluntly*) Suppose you let us hear what Mr. Downright has to communicate. His time I daresay is precious, and so I'm sure is mine.

Down. And cousin Job is right. Let us be seated.
    (*they sit at table*, Downright, c., *facing audience*;
        Harry, R. C.; David, L. C.; Job *front* L., Tompkins, R.)

Now, cousins, we are about to part, and I trust that during my absence you will find things go on as pleasantly and agreeably as when I had my friend Tompkins to assist me. I can only regret that he declines remaining in the counting house, and so I make no doubt, do you.

David. }
Harry. } Oh, sir, of course we do!

Job. Do you? humph! Mr. Downright, as I observed my time is precious. (*looks at his watch*)

Down. I beg your pardon, cousin Job, I am getting tedious; it is the fault of old age. Everything has been settled except one, and it is for the purpose of requesting your kind co-operation that I meet you here. You are aware that I have a poor relation—I may say that *we* have a poor relation, William Lackwit.

Job. A very poor relation.

DAVID. Poor William Lackwit. Heaven knows I have always wished him well.

HARRY. William Lackwit! My dear cousin, not another word; I shall consider it my duty to look after him. Be easy on that score.

DOWN. He is equally related to all of us, and I am sorry to say has lately met with severe losses. You may, perhaps, think, that *I*, who am reputed to be rich, ought not to apply to you. But I am far from being wealthy: and I am going to America in the hope of recovering a large sum, many thousands which are due to the firm by the heirs of a deceased correspondent. I find that I cannot conveniently assist poor cousin William to the extent he requires, and I recommend him to your kindness. Should I return successful, 1 shall be able to make some provision for him; but should I die, promise me that my poor cousin shall not languish in poverty. Job Downright, as the eldest partner, or I should say, the senior in age, what will you promise?

JOB. Nothing.

DAVID & HARRY. Oh, Job, Job!

DOWN. How is this?

JOB. Exactly so! I never make promises; you may not return, cousin Richard, you may be shipwrecked, or the steamer may be blown up; they blow them up in America, I do believe for amusement. How do I know if the vessel in which you have taken a passage is seaworthy? she may be some old tub, which the underwriters decline to insure, even at fifty per cent.

HARRY. Really, this is too bad, dispiriting Mr. Downright in this shameful way.

DAVID. It is atrocious—perfectly atrocious!

JOB. I daresay you think so. But, Mr. Downright, if it be only *promises* that you require, you cannot have better men than the two gentlemen on either side of you.

DOWN. What do you say, David?

DAVID. That whilst I have a shilling, Will Lackwit shall never want. I should hope the firm of Downright would always be able to assist him.

JOB. Suppose the firm of Downright should fail! such things have happened, you know.

Tomp. The firm of Downright fail! Mr. Job, you have no business to suppose anything of the kind; as if the firm *could* fail.

Job. My good Tompkins, such things have happened within the memory of man, consequently I can promise nothing.

Down. Should William Lackwit want a home at any time, which of you would offer him one?

Harry. Need you ask such a thing? Of course my house is open to him.

David. And mine also. He will be as welcome as though he were my own brother. Though, as I am but a bachelor at present, I cannot boast of a very well regulated home; but my cousin Job, who has a large house and a notable wife, can do more for William than I can.

Job. (*rising*) You forget, gentlemen, that as a married man, I must consult my wife. Cousin Richard, whatever I *can* do I *will* do for William Lackwit. I must hurry away now—but I shall see you again. *Exit*, L.

Tomp. I am afraid, Mr. Downright, that you must not expect much from Mr. Job.

Down. Excuse his rough manners. I think he means well; but I wish he had been more explicit. But to proceed:—I must not forget to mention that I have left my parting instructions with Tompkins, who will tell you what they are. Here is William Lackwit's address; and I can only say that every kindness shewn to him, will be a double kindness to myself.

Enter Robert, L.

Robert. The coach is at the door, sir. (*they all rise*)

Down. Then I must leave you. But I hope to meet you here in about twelve months. Should I never return, you will then open my will.

David. } Oh, my dear cousin!—You will return safely,
Harry. } I am sure.

Down. (*shaking hands with them*) I trust I shall. Meanwhile, I wish you every success. Tompkins will see me on board. Good-bye for the present.

Exit, R., *with* Tompkins.

HARRY. What a sudden whim this is of my respected cousin! I suppose we must humour him. Have you any idea what his will can contain?

DAVID. Not the slightest. That sly fellow Tompkins, he knows all about it; but it is useless to try to pump him.

HARRY. Perfectly so. I hope that Job is no wiser than ourselves.

DAVID. He would have been more civil to Richard had he been in the secret. Do you suppose that Richard is in the least embarassed?

HARRY. Embarrassed—embarrassed! What makes you think so?

DAVID. The behaviour—the very cautious behaviour of cousin Job.

Enter JOB, L.

Bless me, Job, what brings you back? But you are too late—Mr. Downright is gone.

JOB. I know it; I parted with him on board the steamer, "The Good Intent," and if ever a ship belied its name, I should say that was the vessel. I never saw a more villainous-looking tub in the whole course of my experience. I wouldn't insure her, nor consign even a damaged cargo to her. What fool recommended such a worthless craft?

DAVID. (*angrily*) If you must know, sir—*I* did!

JOB. Oh! very thoughtful of you to send your bene-factor away in a leaky vessel!

HARRY. Mr. Job, we don't understand such language.

JOB. Then, cousins, you must be greater simpletons than I take you for. I thought you foolish when you were so lavish of your promises to Richard Downright, respecting that poor spendthrift, William Lackwit. Now I am confirmed in my opinion.

HARRY. What do you mean to insinuate? What do you suspect?

DAVID. Yes; what do you suspect? Come now, cousin Job, as our partner you ought to tell us. Is it anything that can affect our interest—no, no, I mean that affects our dear friend?

JOB. Let us first consider the question of interest, which I presume is naturally of the first importance to each of us.

DAVID. Not to me, sir—you are very much mistaken.

JOB. Am I?

HARRY. Yes, sir; very much mistaken, indeed, when you judge us according to your own standard and your own feelings.

JOB. We need not quarrel, Harry; I merely say that I prefer payment, and performance, to promises. Let us dispute no further. Here comes Mr. Tompkins, with more last words for us.

Enter TOMPKINS, L.

Well, Mr. Tompkins, what news?

TOMP. Our respected friend has left us. The " Good Intent" has left the pier, and is steaming down the river. By-the-bye, gentlemen, I have a few words to say to you before we part.

HARRY. They will be as binding to me as a bond.

DAVID. And the same to me.

JOB. Let us hear what you have to say, Tompkins, for it is nearly post time. I must hurry away.

TOMP. I shall not detain you long, gentlemen. But to proceed—it is Mr. Downright's wish that you should not communicate with him during his absence. He will write to the firm when he arrives in America, and also when he returns to England.

HARRY. Very strange! Are we to hear nothing of our respected benefactor during that time?

DAVID. What a deprivation it will be.

JOB. Go on, Mr. Tompkins, or else I must leave you to tell the remainder of my cousin's wishes to my two partners.

TOMP. I really beg pardon. Well, the last wishes of my respected benefactor are, that his cousin, your poor relation, should find a home with some of you. Which of you three gentlemen will undertake the charge of him? Mr. Job, what say you?

JOB. That I shall consult my wife, and think about it —but you may give me his address.

Tomp. Here it is, sir, and I feel sure that you will do what you can for that poor Mr. William.

Job. Tompkins, you may be a good man of business, but not a man of the world. Never take upon yourself to answer for any man's good intentions. Be guided by his actions, and even then you may be deceived. No, it is to my cousins that I refer you on this occasion. They have promised a great deal. and will doubtless keep their word. I wish you good morning.

Exit, L.

David. What, is he gone—really gone?

Harry. It looks uncommonly like it. He has certainly disappeared through the doorway; and I do not imagine that he has any intention of returning, either down the chimney or in at the window.

David. Very strange conduct! and as he is the head of the firm, nothing ought to be done—in fact, nothing can be done without consulting him.

Tomp. But, Mr. David, this is not a matter of business —it is quite an affair of private charity.

David. Pardon me, Mr. Tompkins, this is *not* a paltry private affair; the honor of the firm of Downright is concerned, and whatever *is* done *shall* be done handsomely. I shall bring the subject formally before the firm.

Tomp. And in the meantime, sir——

David. I wish you good morning—you shall hear from me shortly.

Exit, L.

Tomp. It strikes me that Mr. David can also find it convenient to make his way out at the door, as well as Mr. Job.

Harry. Ha, ha, ha! poor David—he very quickly takes offence; but I must hurry after him, or in the heat of the moment he may refuse to do anything.

Tomp. But yourself, Mr. Harry——

Harry. Oh, of course I shall consent to whatever the firm proposes. Good-bye, Tompkins—I shall be delighted to see you whenever you come my way. Good-bye.

Exit, door, L.

Tomp. Either that door possesses great attraction, or else I have been a very bad advocate. Now what am I to say to Mr. Richard?

Enter ROBERT, L.

Well, Robert, what brings you here?

ROBERT. A letter—or I should rather say a parcel for you, sir: and the messenger who brought it would neither tell me who he was, nor where he came from. (*gives parcel and exit,* L.)

TOMP. What can this mysterious parcel be? (*opens it*) Ha! a note addressed to me, and in a female handwriting, or else in that of a very weak-minded male. (*reads*) "Mr. Tompkins is requested (by one who knows his trustworthiness) to employ the enclosed sum in relieving the necessities of Mr. Lackwit, to whom the writer is unknown. The numbers of the notes have been retained." Oh, indeed! well then I can't steal them. But what are they? (*opens a folded paper*) Can I believe my eyes!—a hundred pounds in five-pound notes! Who can this unknown benefactor be? I would give—yes, I *would* give five pounds to find out.

Enter RICHARD DOWNRIGHT, *from a closet—he comes behind* TOMPKINS, *and slaps him on the back.*

DOWN. And I would give ten to find out.

TOMP. Mercy on us, Mr. Downright! What! are you here? What has become of the " Good Intent?"

DOWN. She has been telegraphed to return. I came back, and from that closet have heard every word of the conversation between you—Cautious Cousin Job, Dashing David, and Hearty Harry.

TOMP. What is your opinion of them, sir?—I pronounce them to be three humbugs.

DOWN. So do not I; but I must return on board before I am missed, and before any one knows that I have been on shore. We can slip out unperceived—it is almost dusk. Come along, Tompkins, and you shall have the benefit of some more last words. *Exeunt,* R.

[A Year is supposed to have elapsed since Scene First.]

PART THE SECOND.

SCENE.—*As before—a writing table with account books, chairs, &c., in* C.

JOB, *at writing table.*

JOB. Two and seven make nine—and six, fifteen—and three, eighteen. Eighteen hundred pounds, the profits of the last six weeks;—that is not bad for young beginners. I think my cousin Richard would be satisfied. By the way, where can my two partners be? David had returned from 'Change, and Harry was giving audience to his tailor.

Enter DAVID, L.

DAVID. Well, Job, have you finished the accounts? What do you make the sum total to be?

JOB. The clear profits are eighteen hundred. Are you not content?

DAVID. Yes—I suppose that we ought not to grumble.

JOB. Grumble! when you are in a fair way of making your fortune. Where is Harry?

DAVID. He is coming—I hear him on the stairs. Here he is.

Enter HARRY, R., *he flings his hat down on the table.*

What is the matter, Harry?

HARRY. What's the matter? Why that stupid blockhead the tailor has lost my measure. I must go to the races to-morrow, and have no coat fit to wear.

JOB. What a calamity, Harry! Shall you be able to survive it?

HARRY. (*angrily*) Sir—Mr. Job! Pshaw! it is of no use being angry with an old square-toes like you!

JOB. I think so too. Meanwhile, can you give me your attention to a matter of business?

HARRY. Don't worry me about business, Job. I have betted heavily on the brown colt, Thunderbolt, and can't attend to anything else.

JOB. Oh, indeed! Well, such an important matter as the result of a race must claim precedence. (*closes his book—rises*) I have just received a note from Mr. Tompkins, who is coming here.

DAVID. What ails him? I hope he is all right.

JOB. I hope so; but he communicates with us every six months—and it is just half a year since he wrote to us. I have also received a letter from William Lackwit.

HARRY. From William Lackwit? What makes him turn up just now? I thought that he had been provided for by the firm.

JOB. If you remember, neither yourself nor David came to any decision; so *I* could do nothing in the name of the firm.

HARRY. He has had his annuity?

JOB. Of two pounds a week; just what you tell me your groom costs you: and he has a son to support—for he very honourably gave up all to his creditors. However, Tompkins will be better able to tell us the particulars, (*a knock without*) and here he is, as punctual as clockwork.

Enter TOMPKINS, *door* L.

TOMP. Good-morning, gentlemen.

DAVID. You bring us news of our dear cousin Richard —good news, I hope?

TOMP. I trust that it is good news. In the first place, he is coming back very soon.

HARRY. ⎫
DAVID. ⎬ Coming back! Coming home!

JOB. To thank us, no doubt, for the care we have bestowed on the two trusts he confided to us; namely, the firm, and poor cousin William.

TOMP. The firm, I know, is in the most flourishing condition; and I am convinced that Mr. Downright's wishes respecting his poor relation have been attended to, particularly after the promises you made.

JOB. If you remember, *I* made none, Mr. Tompkins.

TOMP. No, Mr. Job, you did not. I allude to these gentlemen.

HARRY. Why, you see, Tompkins, this has been a busy year with us. Since we saw you, we have both married. Besides, William Lackwit has never applied to us—at least I have heard nothing of it if he has.

JOB. I beg your pardon; Mr. Lackwit wrote repeatedly to ask us if we could find employment for his son. You would not consent to receive him into our counting-house.

HARRY. Heavens, David! what do I hear? You refused to admit the son of William Lackwit into the counting-house, where of course there ought to be a desk for him.

JOB. Harry, I am afraid that *oughts* here *do* stand for nothing. Tompkins, in what vessel does my cousin Richard take his passage.

TOMP. He returns by the first that sails; but has already sent good bills by the last mail. He has received considerable sums.

DAVID. Has Mr. Downright been fortunate in America?

TOMP. He has unexpectedly recovered several thousands which he had long given up as lost.

HARRY. (*aside*) I'll send fifty pounds directly to William Lackwit. What a fool I was not to think of that before!

DAVID. (*aside*) I will invite William Lackwit to dinner. That will be sure to please Richard. I wish I had done so long ago!

JOB. (*takes up paper*) "The Good Intent," you said, is the vessel in which Richard was to sail? Let me see if there are any tidings of her in the papers of to-day. Here we are—" Shipping Intelligence." Ha, what is this? (*reads*) "We are sorry to learn that a vessel, which has since been ascertained to be 'The Good Intent,' sprang a leak when off the Scilly Isles, and foundered. Every soul on board perished."

RICHARD. ⎱
DAVID. ⎰ Impossible! our dear cousin Richard!

TOMP. Is dead! Alas, can this be true?

JOB. I fear it is. You know that I had my doubts respecting the "Good Intent"—I told you so, David.

TOMP. What ought to be done now? I came here, hoping in a few days to meet my friend and benefactor. Alas! I can now only fulfil his last instructions, namely, to read his will!

JOB. There will be no hurry, Mr. Tompkins. I am scarcely equal to hearing it now.

DAVID. Cousin Job, would you dispute the last wishes of that excellent man?

HARRY. Over whose remains we cannot have the melancholy pleasure of weeping, nor of consigning them to the silent tomb.

JOB. Be it as you choose then—I will not dispute your will. (*sits*)

TOMP. I think I had better go and bring the will. I shall not be long, gentlemen. Alas, my poor friend!

Exit, L.

DAVID. I need not write yet to William Lackwit.

HARRY. No; it would be advisable to hear the will first. Do you not think so, Job?

JOB. About William Lackwit—ah, of course. It is quite right that he should be present. He is in town, I know; and I have written to request that he will call at Mr. Richard Downright's, where I appointed to meet him.

DAVID. Indeed! I must say, cousin Job, that you have done very wrong. None of us have ever seen William Lackwit, not even yourself. He is a perfect stranger to us.

JOB. He stands in the same degree of relationship to the deceased Mr. Downright as we do. It is only right that he should be present at the reading of the will, which, I must say, need not have taken place the very moment we heard of Richard's death. As you force me to be present, you must accept of the company of our poor relation as well.

HARRY. (*with a sneer*) You expect to be sole legatee, and wish to give a touching proof of affection for poor Richard's memory—love me, love my dog. It is sometimes convenient to fawn on the cur we have previously spurned, and to extend the same kindness to all the whelps of the litter.

JOB. If you have abused me sufficiently, Harry, let us change the subject, and be friends, in appearance.

Enter TOMPKINS, L., *and an* ELDERLY MAN *in spectacles; a tie-wig, and shabby great coat.*

TOMP. Gentlemen—permit me to introduce your cousin, Mr. William Lackwit.

JOB. (*shaking* LACKWIT *by the hand*) I am happy to see you, cousin William; but could have wished that our meeting had taken place under different circumstances.

LACK. (*bowing stiffly*) Mr. Job, I am greatly obliged to you.

HARRY. (*aside to* DAVID) The old fellow has certain expectations, he is so deuced haughty. (*to* LACKWIT) I need not say, cousin, how happy I shall be to serve you.

DAVID. And I beg to be included in the number of your friends.

LACK. Have the poor any friends? I think it is very doubtful. What say you, cousin Job?

JOB. That friends become scarcer every day; I think the race must be almost extinct. But let us proceed to business, since we are here : cousin William, I requested your presence in order that you might learn the contents of our late cousin's will, which Mr. Tompkins is now going to read. (*they all sit*—TOMPKINS *in the centre*)

TOMP. (*breaking the seal of the will and glancing over it*) This is the will—the new will, dated the day before the American mail sailed, and now opened for the first time; in it my dear friend states that the bulk of his fortune he had already disposed of, in various bequests. But there still remains a further sum, the amount of which his executor, myself, will distribute between the three gentlemen who now represent the firm of Downright.

HARRY. Dear cousin Richard! he was ever considerate.

DAVID. The bequest is in ready money, I suppose.

TOMP. In ready money; you can receive it to-morrow if you will. One-fifth of the sum is to be handed over to Mr. Job Downright, the remainder to be equally divided between Messrs Harry and David, because, as the testator observes, they so generously promised to take care of our relation William Lackwit.

DAVID. It is most generous, and what we had no right to expect.

JOB. (*after a pause*) Has nothing been left to Mr. William Lackwit.

TOMP. I regret to say nothing, not even the annuity I had orders to pay him. Mr. Richard relies entirely on the promises made by his generous cousins.

HARRY. And not in vain; we shall certainly continue the annuity between us.

DAVID. Most certainly we shall continue the annuity.

JOB. And what do you intend to do for the son; you really can afford to be generous.

DAVID. The son whom you chose to take under your special protection, Mr. Job, we decline to interfere with.

HARRY. Yes, we altogether decline—and as to the father, we shall be guided by circumstances.

DAVID. Yes entirely by circumstances. Pray what are your own liberal intentions, Job? (*they all rise*)

JOB. I made no promise, but if my cousin William can put up with our plain living, our quiet mode of life, and he does not object to young children, of which I have a housefull, he is heartily welcome to consider my home as his home also. And I shall take care that part of my cousin's handsome legacy shall be set apart to give young William a start in life. Cousins, those are my intentions.

TOMP. Mr. Job, you are a brave, noble-hearted fellow! I wronged you; I always thought you were cold and calculating.

JOB. Because I am not profuse in promises; they are unsafe things to deal in. And now let us adjourn to my house. Cousin William, you must make the acquaintance of my good wife. Tompkins, you will dine with us. I could not presume, David and Harry, to ask you to join our party.

HARRY. Thank you, Job—I am engaged.

DAVID. And so am I; I promised to to take Mrs. Downright to the concert.

JOB. But not to-night, I should hope.

Enter ROBERT, *hastily*, L., *with a note, which he hands to* JOB.

ROBERT. A note from a gentleman who wishes to see you.

JOB. Shew the gentleman in.   *Exit* ROBERT, L.
But who can he be? (*opens note*) Hey-day—it is signed William Lackwit senior; who can he be?

B

Enter ROBERT, *showing in* WILLIAM LACKWIT, L.

ROBERT. Mr. William Lackwit. *Exit* ROBERT., *door* L.

JOB. What, my cousin William.

LACK. The same to whom your bounty has been so liberally distributed. Ah, cousin Job! you are found out: your wife has let out the secret of the hundred pounds which I received the day after my cousin Richard had sailed. I taxed her with having written the note which accompanied it. Bless you I knew the handwriting again when I received her kind invitation. I have just arrived here—I went first to your house, found that you were not at home, and am come after you to thank you for your kindness to the "Poor Relation."

JOB. So you have found me out! I never felt so foolish in all my life. But if you are William Lackwit, who is our friend here, whom Mr. Tompkins introduced to us under your name?

HARRY. Oh some impostor no doubt. I wish you joy, cautious cousin Job, of the new acquaintance who is to share your home.

. DAVID. (*to* STRANGER) I shall insist, fellow, on knowing who and what you are. Tompkins, I shall hold you answerable for this person.

TOMP. I am perfectly willing, Mr. David, to answer for him.

(STRANGER *throwing off the wig, great coat, and spectacles, discovers himself to be* RICHARD DOWNRIGHT)

DOWN. No; let me rather answer for myself.

OMNES. Richard Downright!

HARRY. Not dead!

RICHARD. No, alive.

DAVID. You didn't go down then, cousin?

RICHARD. No, I changed my mind, and came over in the same steamer which brought my money. But I find that my unexpected arrival has disconcerted you.—Why Harry, David, how crestfallen you appear.

HARRY. Mr. Richard, this has been an infamous vile plot to entrap us.

DAVID. Yes, and Mr. Tompkins, I shall expect the satisfaction of a gentleman from you.

TOMP. Mr. David, I am too old to think of such tom-foolery as duels. Is it my fault that you have shewn yourself in your true colours?

DAVID. Oh, defend yourself, sir! you and Mr. Job there were in league to—to—to insult me. *Exit in a rage*, R.

JOB. Poor David, he *is* vexed!

HARRY. Vexed; I should think so. I shall not remain here with such a hypocrite, you have behaved shamefully, sir! *Exit angrily*, R.

JOB. I must be signally and singularly wicked, to have incurred their anger! Cousin Richard, need I say how glad I am to see you? believe me, I mean it.

DOWN. I know you do; I misjudged you, and so did Tompkins; but I know your worth, your noble behaviour to our kinsman.

JOB. Pooh, Pooh! don't make me out to be a miracle of virtue; I merely carried out your favourite proverb: "Love me—love my dog."

DOWN. Upon my word, fortune did behave as badly to William Lackwit as though he had been one. But now I trust, that here end the troubles and ill-luck of "The Poor Relation."

JOB.   DOWNRIGHT.

TOMPKINS.   LACKWIT.

R.   L.

Curtain.

THE TALISMAN;

OR,

" TRUTH MAY BE BLAMED, BUT IT CANNOT BE SHAMED."

An original Drama,

IN ONE ACT.

FOR MALE CHARACTERS ONLY.

THOMAS HAILES LACY,

89, STRAND,

(*Opposite Southampton Street, Covent Garden Market,*)

LONDON.

Characters.

PRINCE FLORIMOND ....

THE BARON ST. VALLERY (*former Tutor to Florimond*) ....

BEAUCHATEAU ⎫

CLARIFORT...... ⎬ (*young Courtiers*) ... ⎰

MONTCLAIR ... ⎭

ANDRE (*an Under-Gardener*) ....

THE SPIRITS OF THE WOOD..............

Scene.—In the Gardens of the Palace.

Costumes—ABOUT 1750.

PRINCE.—Elegant crimson embroidered velvet coat and breeches, white satin waistcoat, white silk stockings, shoes with red heels, paste buckles, lace cravat and ruffles, powder, three-cornered hat with gold lace and feather trimmings, sword.

THE OTHER NOBLES.—Dresses of the same character, but differing in colour, and not so rich.

ANDRE.—Round jacket, long waistcoat, full breeches, grey stockings, black shoes, apron, flaxen hair, straw hat.

SPIRIT.—White satin shirt, trimmed with flowers and jewels, flesh leggings, spangled sandals, long hair, and wreath of flowers and jewels.

THE TALISMAN.

—◦◦{◦}◦◦—

SCENE.—*Gardens of the Palace, beautifully laid out;
fountains, flowers, vases, statues, &c.*

Enter ST. VALLERY *and* FLORIMOND, R.

ST. VAL. Am I to understand that your highness
really wishes me to remain here?

FLORI. Yes; for are you not, my dear baron, my best
friend and counsellor!

ST. VAL. I certainly have the honour of being *consulted*
occasionally.

FLORI. I know what you would say; I consult you,
but seldom follow your advice.

ST. VAL. I cannot accuse your highness of having
often done so.

FLORI. Oh, you must not be vexed; remember that
times and opinions have changed since you were young.

ST. VAL. They have indeed! you need not remind me
of it, Prince.

FLORI. We should be supremely ridiculous if we introduced the obsolete customs and manners of those good
old times.   Do you not think so?

ST. VAL. I think that many of your young friends
possess the talent of being, as you term it, supremely
ridiculous, without having recourse to what you term
obsolete customs and manners.

FLORI. We shall never agree, my dear lord, therefore
let us not dispute.   But why have you taken such a
violent dislike to my companions, those three young
noblemen, who have followed me hither?

LT. VAL. Possibly because I think them the very three
whom you should *not* have selected.   Listen patiently,
Prince Florimond, to your old tutor.   You are very young,
inexperienced, guileless, rather vain of your knowledge of

A 2

human nature, of which you know very little, and of men in general, of whom you know less——

FLORI. You are not very complimentary.

ST. VAL. I hope not, truth-tellers seldom are; that is if they really respect those whom they profess and wish to serve. Young as you are, the king, your august father, wishes by degrees to initiate you into the secrets and duties of governing a state. He has appointed you viceroy of this distant province which has recently become annexed to his rich and vast domains. He trusts that your kindly nature, your pleasing manners, and frank, generous disposition will reconcile his new subjects to their new monarch; you have had absolute power here for a month. May I ask what good you have already done?

FLORI. I have scarcely had time to do much. On my first arrival, you must agree, that I was so overwhelmed with fétes, balls, and grand receptions, that I had very little time left for business.

ST. VAL. Oh, I am well aware that such trifles as affairs of state, the happiness and prosperity of some millions of inhabitants, must give way to the more important claims of masked balls, banquets, illuminations, hunting parties, and pastoral ballets, where lords and ladies are so beautifully and correctly dressed, that one might imagine the wand of an enchanter had animated a collection of rare chinaware figures, in fact all the Chloes, Damons, Pastoras, and Colins that ever existed in the poet's imagination, or were fashioned in a porcelain manufactory.

FLORI. You are very severe on modern amusements, my dear tutor, at the same time I feel you are right; it *is* a foolish waste of time, and from this very day I will reform. No more lavish expenditure, no more fétes, of which to tell you the truth, I am becoming rather weary. I will follow your advice—attend to my duties. I will call a cabinet council this morning.

ST. VAL. The Duke de Beauchateau, whom you appointed president may not be at liberty, to attend to it, I heard that he was arranging, and superintending the concert for to-night; at which some of the compositions of your royal highness are to be played for the first time.

FLORI. True, I had forgotten that. I must not disappoint Beauchateau, my best friend, a young man of such merit and accomplishments.

ST. VAL. And who would make a first-rate flute player, for which I think nature intended him. Whether he can preside with equal ability at a council of state I am not yet competent to judge.

FLORI. (*pettishly*) He at least will conciliate, for Beauchateau is never contradictory or peremptory; at least to me. Well then to-morrow be it, as early as you like to assemble.

ST. VAL. The young Count de Clarifort, your master of the horse and grand huntsman, has issued a notice that a royal stag hunt will take place to-morrow, at which all the court, the ladies included, will be present in the new uniform; in the choice of which you have shewn so much good taste.

FLORI. I cannot disappoint two or three hundred people, but I promise you the day after. Oh! I had forgotten— Montclair had arranged for a private rehearsal of the allegorical masque I wrote.

ST. VAL. Which you wrote, with the assistance of your poet laureate. I will no longer intrude.

FLORI. Intrude! that you never can, my dear baron, only I——

ST. VAL. You are so used to the flattery and fine speeches of these young men, that my plain-spoken truths are unpalatable. But I perceive that one of your principal ministers is coming: I take my leave for the present.

Bows, and exit, R. 1 E.

FLORI. How provoking to be compelled to listen to him, and to feel too that he is right, for something tells me that I am not following the path I ought to tread; a life of mere pleasure, and amusement, innocent though it may be, it is not the one for which my sire destined me; And yet there can be no great wrong in it after all. Every one tells me so : and what every one says must be true.

Enter BEAUCHATEAU, *laughing,* L. U. E.

BEAUCHATEAU. My dear prince—pardon my hilarity— but I cannot help laughing.

FLORI. What occasions your mirth?

BEAU. Imagine your highness, that just as we were in the middle of the rehearsal of the battle piece of your composition, (which is really a master-piece), that remarkably grave person, the private secretary of the prime minister, had the impertinence to request that we would be quiet; as it was impossible either for him, or any of the gentlemen in his office to attend to business while so much noise was going on. The concert room, you know, is close to the secretary's suite of apartments.

FLORI. But of course you complied——

BEAU. I desired the orchestra to repeat the finale *con strepito*, and with all the force they could command. Does your highness imagine that I would allow such a covert insult to yourself to pass unnoticed? No, indeed! I was honoured with your commands and was determined they should be obeyed.

FLORI. Still, my dear Beauchateau, if the secretary should be in the right.

BEAU. Which he was not: I can prove that he was decidedly in the wrong. Recollect that as the viceroy here, your word is law; and if once your ministers find that they rule you, instead of you ruling them, adieu to your authority: you had better abdicate at once. No, your highness must shew them you are not the puppet they take you for.

FLORI. Oh as to that, I can be firm, as you well know.

BEAU. I know you can, and I trust that you approve of my zeal. Ha! here come Clarifort and Montclair.

FLORI. Just in time. I wish to consult them about the new masque, and the grand stag hunt; for after those two fêtes have been given, I must really attend a little more to business; St. Vallery is right.

Enter CLARIFORT *and* MONTCLAIR, L.

Good morning, my dear friends.

CLARI. Your highness, I have been seeking for you everywhere; there is business of the greatest importance which cannot be settled till we have had your opinion.

FLORI. Indeed! what is this very important business?

MONT. One in which every person of taste is interested; the new uniform for the royal hunt, and the colour of the dresses for the masque and ballet. Imagine that there are barbarians who object to the quality of the material we had selected.

FLORI. Had we not decided on a rich green and gold for the huntsmen, and scarlet and silver for the court.

CLARI. But that miserly old marquis, who has hitherto been lord treasurer, objects to the green and gold; and suggests that plain brown minus the gold would be more serviceable. He even refused to pay the tailor's bills, that I ordered to be sent to him, unless your highness commanded him to do so.

FLORI. But I understood, Clarifort, that the new liveries were to be made at my own expense. The king gave me a large sum when I took leave of him. It was intended to defray the expenses of my civil list for some time.

MONT. Your royal highness has been so very profuse in your bounty that I fear there is little of the original sum left. Clarifort is Chancellor of the Exchequer and will tell you how much remains.

CLARI. A couple of thousand crowns.

FLORI. I have spent then, nearly half a million of crowns in four weeks, and on what?

CLARI. They will be easily accounted for; you have given largely to artists of all descriptions, then fêtes, and balls, and banquets cost something.

FLORI. Those follies I hope are paid for!

CLARI. All except the grand concert and the masque, but the expense will be trifling. A word from you, prince, will compel this closefisted treasurer to unlock the coffers of the state and furnish you with money. Oh! apropos, I must not forget to say that the ladies who act in the masque have selected pink as the most becoming colour, in preference to pale yellow; and the gentlemen will appear in white and blue. But really, my dear prince, you have a most dejected air!

FLORI. Clarifort, I am thinking that this lavish expense has been uncalled for. How am I to pay my servants— relieve the poor, if I continue at this rate!

MONT. Oh, we shall find means. A young viceroy must

be generous! But will not your highness come and inspect the preparations for the masque?

CLARI. And above all we must try on our new dresses.

BEAU. Do not forget, prince, that you promised to go over that battle piece with me.

FLORI. I will be with you immediately—at present I really must be left to myself a little. I will join you in a few minutes.

(BEAUCHATEAU; CLARIFORT *and* MONTCLAIR *bow, and exeunt,* L.)

Is it possible that I have already erred and have involved myself. I relied too implicitly on the assertions of my young friends, and consequently I am already deeply in debt. I, who promised my excellent father that nothing should induce me to launch out into extravagance. Would that it were possible for princes always to know the truth; I have been terribly misled. (*music*)

The SPIRIT OF THE WOOD *suddenly appears from a bush,* R.

SPIRIT. Prince Florimond, the wish you have uttered with such sincerity, I shall be delighted to gratify.

FLORI. Who are you, fair child? I never remember having seen you before.

SPIRIT. You have not. I prefer the seclusion of these leafy woods and blooming gardens to all the glitter of a court. We have not met before, and I fear that many of the fine ladies and gentlemen who surround you, would gladly dispense with my company; but although personally I am unknown to you, I am not unacquainted with you.

FLORI. You surprise me, how can that be?

SPIRIT. To me it is quite possible; I have often watched you, when engaged in the pursuit of pleasure here, or when amused with the witticisms of your youthful ministers; besides, I overheard your conversation with your former tutor, and also that with which your three officers of state regaled you; I must own the latter was not quite as instructive as the former.

FLORI. Where could you have concealed yourself?

SPIRIT. What matters it that you should know? perhaps I was concealed in the cup of yonder lily, or hidden beneath that modest violet, or else I nestled within the leaves of the moss rose. I will not puzzle you any longer; will you obey my directions, and act as I shall bid you, if I promise that you for once *shall hear the truth* from all? Are you prepared to accept this offer?

FLORI. I am, and I place implicit faith in your words.

SPIRIT. You will have no reason to regret the confidence you repose in me. Prince, if you would learn the truth, I can present you with a talisman, which has the power of obliging those on whom you bestow it, to speak of you as unreservedly as though you were not present, and at the same time to be unconscious of what they are saying. Here is a rose—here a carnation, a pansey, and a sprig of mignionette; bestow them with discretion, and when we next meet, perhaps you may thank me for the lesson you have received. Adieu, Florimond, for the present. *Exit*, R.

FLORI. That surely must be some benign fairy: I shall not be afraid to make use of my talisman. But on whom shall I try its effects?—on St. Vallery?—no, it would be useless: he speaks the truth always, and sometimes rather harshly. I am certain of the affection of Beauchateau, Clarifort, and Montclair, my three favourites, as they are called. We were boys together, they are sincerely attached to me, and I feel certain they will stand the test. Ah! who comes here? A peasant lad, whom I have seen working occasionally in the gardens. He appears to be in trouble; I'll stand aside, and watch him. *Exit*, R. U. E.

Enter ANDRE *with a watering pot and rake*, L.

ANDRE. Heigho! what a life of toil I do lead; nothing but work! work! and at the year's end, I am just as poor as ever. Now, I put it to any reasonable being, what is the use of toiling like a slave? I have made up my mind not to bear it any longer: I'll run away; and then perhaps the great folks here will find out what a capital gardener they have lost. Ah! they told us such fine stories about our new king; and how happy we should be—plenty of work, good wages, and cheap food. I am afraid they have not kept their word, these great folks; except in respect to our hard work: there indeed I'll say that for them, they do give us plenty of hard work, and hard words as well. As to the wages, and cheap food, I'm thinking they have clean forgotten them altogether. (*begins to water the flowers, and rake the beds*)

Re-enter FLORIMOND, R; *he wears a large brown coat, with broad leather belt, and plain hat.*

FLORI. Good morning, friend; you seem very busy at work.

ANDRE. Very busy! Oh! you are a stranger here, I suppose, or you might guess that I had been very busy here for the last seven hours.

FLORI. Indeed! it is scarcely noonday yet! Have you been working since five in the morning?

ANDRE. I was here shortly after sunrise; and I shall be at work here, till sunset.

FLORI. What is your employment here, friend?

ANDRE. I am under-gardener to one of the deputy under-gardeners, so please you, sir.

FLORI. Have you lived here long?

ANDRE. I have worked here ever since I could handle a spade, and knew a rose from a cauliflower.

FLORI. You are most likely a good florist. I have just met with a new specimen of pansy: I think it rather curious, for I have never seen one like it. (*gives* ANDRE *the pansy*)

ANDRE. (*examines pansy*) Nor I! May I be so bold as to ask if you gathered it here, sir?

FLORI. I did not: but pray keep it; perhaps you have a love for rare flowers.

ANDRE. Thank ye, sir—I will keep it. (*sticks it in his button-hole*) I am sure if there is anything I can do for you——

FLORI. You can tell me something respecting the young viceroy, whom your new king has sent to govern here.

ANDRE. Then, it is little I know of him, except by hearsay. Bless you, I have never seen him.

FLORI. I thought, that when the prince made his public entry into the city, that every one saw him?

ANDRE. Yes; every one who was well dressed, and had the courage to push themselves forward. As to me, I only saw the tip of his royal highness's cocked-hat, and the tail of his horse : and, though I hurrahed as loud as I could, I was thrust back by the guards.

FLORI. But, if you have had no opportunity of seeing the prince, I hope that you are satisfied with his government?

ANDRE. Aye, if a poor man could live on sight-seeing, and reviews, and hearing about fêtes, and fine doings that are going on. But, instead of all these balls, and feasts, and tomfoolery, I wish the prince would order our wages to be paid us regularly.

FLORI. Is it possible that a poor peasant, like yourself, can be kept without the pittance he earns?

ANDRE. You see, sir, we are paid by our masters, the head gardeners, if they do not get money, how can we expect they will give it us?

(ST. VALLERY *appears at back, and listens*)

FLORI. The prince cannot know anything of this!

ANDRE. How should he? *He* never troubles himself about the people, the poor, and the hard-working fellows like me. If he did, do you think, sir, he would do nothing but amuse himself, and spend money on pleasure, and finery, and nonsense, and let us starve or nigh it?

FLORI. I do not think he would. Has no one the courage to speak to him to tell him the truth?

ANDRE. Tell him the truth! Pshaw! I should like to see the man who would dare to do it. Ah, if our young prince—Ah, bless him! I say, and make him as good a man as his father!—if he knew but the half they say of him now, he would soon turn over a new leaf. Why look ye, sir, he has only been here a month, and I'll be hanged if everything is not topsy-turvey. I expect every day to be turned out, because I can't make the pinks and boxes grow fast enough to please the ladies and gentlemen of the court. There's our poor cottage, the roof wants mending, I have no money to pay the thatcher; I just get bread for my old mother and myself. I can tell you, sir, the prince's hounds are better cared for than we are. They talk of laying on a new tax; a fine thing for those who can scarcely make both ends meet. But of course we may starve in order that great men may be amused.

FLORI. I hope not; what! shall the honest and industrious

pay for the follies of the heartless and idle? Why do you not complain to the prince himself? Go boldly to him; it is his duty to listen to the poor as well as to the rich, to repair a wrong done to the lowliest, as promptly as he would resent an injury to himself.

ANDRE. (*laughing*) You'll excuse the liberty I take, sir, but you must be very simple indeed, if you think that any of the fine dressed out fellows about the prince, would let me speak to him, much less tell him the truth, as I have told it to you. I wonder how long my head would keep upon my shoulders (*aside*) Lord, what a simpleton that young fellow must be! I must be going to my work yonder; good day, sir.

FLORI. Stop for one moment. What is your name?

ANDRE. Andre, so please you, sir.

FLORI. Andre—what do you wish for most?

ANDRE. What do I wish for most? Why, that our young prince might just learn how to make good use of his seven senses. But I sometimes think between you and me, sir, that he wants the two best senses of the seven.

FLORI. And what are they? He is neither blind nor deaf, so it cannot be sight nor hearing.

ANDRE. It is as bad though—he wants *common* sense and *good* sense; and our good king might as well have sent us his wig-block by way of a viceroy.

FLORI. Indeed, Andre, I am very much of your opinion as to the prince: he ought to be ashamed of himself for his neglect.

ANDRE. Now don't you go to abuse him. He is not so bad after all; it is only because no one tells him the truth. He believes too easily what other folks say.

FLORI. A prince should see and judge for himself. Well, Andre, what do you most wish for, for yourself? You seem to me a good, honest lad, and I should like to serve you. I have not been here long—but I have some little influence at court.

ANDRE. Have you, sir? Then how I do wish that the prince would be pleased to make me one of his upper gardeners for life, and let me have a good warm house to live in, and wages regularly paid. Who knows but that in time I should be able to buy a cow, and keep pigs and poultry! It would take a long time though to do that! I should say it would take years before I could scrape together sixty crowns.

FLORI. Who knows but what Prince Florimond may grant your wish—I will speak a good word for you. Are you now going to your work?

FLORI. Yes, sir—in the rose-walk yonder. I shall be at work there till evening.

FLORI. I will send a friend for you;—will you come with him?—and I can safely promise that the prince shall befriend you.

ANDRE. The prince, say you? What, you know him very well?

FLORI. Perhaps not much better than you do; but sufficiently so, to feel assured that if *I* speak to him, he will do something for you.

ANDRE. I'll come, sir—never fear! Who knows but that I shall be a lucky fellow, after all? *Exit*, L. U. E.

FLORI. Poor fellow! can such a trifle make him happy? —work, a life of labour, and sixty crowns. Alas! I ordered two hundred to be given to a poet, who wrote a complimentary ode on me; the verses were execrable, but I was told that princes must be generous.

ST. VALLERY *comes forward*, R.

St. Vallery, are you here? I thought that you were engaged with my ministers at this hour.

ST. VAL. With your father's ministers, I suppose you mean? No; your highness having postponed the meeting of the council, I had no business to transact with them to-day. But you appear dejected—what has occurred to dispirit you?

FLORI. I have been seriously thinking over what you told me this morning.

ST. VAL. I am glad to hear it. A serious thought must have become a great novelty to you lately. A young peasant left you just now. Have you been conversing with him?

FLORI. Yes; but I must first tell you of a pleasant adventure that has happened to me. Do you, my dear baron, believe in good and bad spirits?

St. Val. I confess that I am rather sceptical on the subject. Why do you ask me?

Flori. Because, not long since, a beautiful boy, the Spirit of the Wood, suddenly appeared before me, as if in answer to my wish.

St. Val. May I ask, prince, what was your wish?

Flori. You may, for it was one to which you would not have objected. I wished *that I might hear the truth from all who surround me.* Scarcely were the words uttered, than this good genius appeared to me, and presented me with four flowers—assuring me that on whomever I bestowed them, those persons would be compelled to speak the truth, and that too without being aware of it. I have already tried the effect of one flower, and I am convinced of its virtue.

St. Val. And on whom did you make the experimeut?

Flori. Truly, on the peasant with whom I spoke. He was not aware of my rank; and he told me so many truths, that it will be long ere I can pardon the want of thought I have shewn, or my careless and cold indifference to the duties of my station.

St. Val. So a few minutes' conversation with an un-educated country lad has really worked a change in your sentiments.

Flori. He spoke the words of truth, and I felt the force of all he said. Oh, my dear St. Vallery! how unfit am I to rule others when I cannot even govern my own caprices. Could you believe it!—I have squandered half a million of crowns in little more than a month.

St. Val. I am sorry to say that I can believe it; and what is still worse, you have given the enemies and opponents of Government reason for spreading all sorts of unfavourable reports. They foretel increased taxes, a ruinous price for provisions, misery and starvation, if this expenditure increases or even continues.

Flori. It shall not—I feel that I am on the edge of an abyss—my friends are not aware of it.

St. Val. You mean the three young gentlemen against whom I took the liberty of warning your highness. Ah! a happy thought strikes me. Prince Florimond, you shall try the effect of these flowers on your so-called friends.

FLORI. Oh, no! I cannot doubt their truth. Beauchateau, for instance, is the soul of candour—you have often heard him contradict me.

ST. VAL. When you have condemned a folly of your own, in which he had been a participator, then he has been very energetic in proving that you were perfectly in the right. Prince—I ask it as a favour—put these young men to the proof. I do not wish you to subject them to the same trial you did that rude-spoken peasant. Give me these magic flowers—these floral talismans—I will present one to each of the three. They are coming here; conceal yourself among those trees and thick flowering shrubs, and perhaps you may hear some more truths from the lips of the young duke and his companions.

FLORI. Is that not very like playing the spy upon them? besides, they say that listeners——

ST. VAL. Never hear any good of themselves. Granted; but you need fear no unpleasant disclosures, secure as you are of the esteem and friendship of your young companions. Besides it will be less humiliating both to you and to them, that the truth should be spoken behind your back, as they will imagine. Come, you must consent;— indulge this whim of mine.

FLORI. It shall be as you please, St. Vallery, here are the precious flowers. (*gives flowers*)

ST. VAL. And I assure you they shall not long be useless. Now to your hiding place, for here comes one of the two. (FLORIMOND *conceals himself behind a clump of flowering shrubs*, R.) I foretel that much good may arise from the rencontre with the Spirit of the Wood.

Enter BEAUCHATEAU, *singing*, L. 1 E.

Good morning, duke! you appear very gay. Are state affairs such amusing things?

BEAU. State affairs! Upon my word I have not thought much about them. I am at present more pleasantly engaged in superintending the arrangements for the concert of this evening. Do you know, Baron St. Vallery, where I can find the prince? He was here just now.

ST. VAL. He was, and he commissioned me to present

you with this rose, and to request that you would do him the favour of wearing it. (*gives the rose to* BEAUCHATEAU, *who places it in his button hole*) I have business to transact for his highness. So now, duke, I must leave you. *Exit*, L.

BEAU. What a tiresome old twaddler he is! and I strongly suspect him of poisoning the mind of the prince. However, I shall be on my guard against all his machinations.

Enter CLARIFORT *and* MONTCLAIR, L. U. E.

Ah! Clarifort—Montclair, so you are there! Can you tell me where the prince has hidden himself?

CLARI. Not I, truly! I have had enough of his company for this morning. Ah! how weary I am! Apropos, duke, what is the meaning of this sprig of mignionette which Florimond insists on my wearing.

MONT. And I have a carnation, which I presume is to be my emblem flower for a time, Well, how are we to get through the day, eh, Beauchateau? Why you look as tired and blasé, as though you had already been presiding at a council of state.

BEAU. Worse than that, Montclair; I have been endeavouring to put something like music and harmony into that unfortunate battlepiece which we are to inflict this evening on the court. I would strongly recommend all the company to provide themselves with night caps, for they will certainly fall asleep in the middle of it.

MONT. I always heard you pronounce it to be a masterpiece of composition.

BEAU. Of stupidity, you mean; it has neither melody, science, nor harmony—in fact it is merely noise set to music. Of course it would never do to tell the prince point blank that he knows nothing of composition; the court will pronounce the battle piece to be charming, and I shall ever remain first favourite, and who knows, perhaps in time I may be even prime minister.

CLARI. A pretty pair prince and minister would be; and if your protocols are no better than his poetry, I wish you joy of your office.

BEAU. Poetry! oh, you mean the new masque; I have not even heard it read, it has been kept a profound secret from all except the author and the actors.

CLARI. Montclair can tell you more about it; he happens to be one of the principal performers.

MONT. And I shall have the misfortune of repeating some of the most tiresome platitudes that were ever penned. Had not the poet laureate touched up the verses a little, I know not how we should ever have been able to commit such doggrel to memory.

BEAU. Doggrel! why, Montclair, did you not assure the prince that the masque was capitally written?

MONT. Do princes ever hear the truth? I can only say with the great French writer, there certainly is much that is both original and good in the masque; but unfortunately for the young author, what is original is not good, and what is good is not original. Ha, ha, ha!

CLARI. How severe you are upon the future Augustus of the age.

BEAU. And to whom you aspire to become the Mæcenas.

MONT. I—well, I could contrive to be respectable in that office; but poor Clarifort, who is commanded to order such hideous costumes, he who should have been court tailor, for that I am sure is his vocation!

CLARI. Yes, Beauchateau, judge if I have not reason to complain: I had imagined some of the most becoming dresses, when the prince with his usual taste, or rather his usual want of taste, would suggest such alterations and additions, that on my honour our corps dramatique will resemble an ill-made rainbow, a crazy kaleidoscope, or a badly assorted piece of patchwork.

BEAU. Upon my word, Clarifort, you are becoming witty. But if we are to credit you and Montclair, the poor dear prince has neither taste, wit, nor invention; for what then is he calculated?

CLARI. Humph! He may make a decent sort of king, nothing more, believe me.

MONT. And perhaps not a bad legislator.

BEAU. Whilst I am of opinion that he may reign with tolerable credit to himself, though he is an execrable musician. (FLORIMOND comes forward, stands behind

Beauchateau) But he would be dreadfully offended if we were bold enough to tell him so.

Flori. (c., *tapping* Beauchateau's *shoulder*) Indeed, he would not, I can answer for it.

(*they all three start back amazed*)

Beau. (r., *aside*) The Prince, by all that's unlucky!

Clari. (l., *aside*) I am ruined for ever! He has heard every word!

Mont. (l.c., *aside*) The Prince!—Then I may as well ask for my passport, and permission to travel to the Antipodes.

Flori. You all appear dreadfully alarmed at my sudden appearance. Yes, gentlemen, I overheard all you have said; I think you were perfectly right, and I coincide with you in opinion.

Beau. Your highness heard then?——

Flori. Something rather novel—the truth. But do not for one moment imagine that I am vexed. I only wish you had been equally candid long ago, and you would have spared me many regrets for the past.

Enter St. Vallery, l.

Ah, baron, you come in time to assure these gentlemen that I bear them no malice for the truths they have unwittingly said of me in my hearing.

St. Val. What! have you really heard the *truth?* I fear, prince, that it has not been very palatable to you?

Flori. (*laughs*) Well, not at first; for it appears that I am an execrable musician—am devoid of wit or taste. But they do me the favour to say that I may possibly become a good king and an upright legislator. Was it not so? (*to* Beauchateau)

Beau. Your highness, after what has passed, our presence here can be neither agreeable nor desirable. We will take our departure, with your permission. (*crosses*, l.)

Flori. No, stay—be still my friends; only speak always *to* me as fearlessly as you have spoken *of* me.

St. Val. Prince, why should they not? It only requires honesty of purpose to do so. You very likely think those flowers given to you by that mysterious personage, the Spirit of the Wood, had some power in compelling your young friends to be truthful.

FLORI. And had they not?

ST. VAL. Flowers like those would be invaluable in a court. You must forgive your old tutor for a little artifice of which he has been guilty.

FLORI. Why surely you have not been playing me a trick.

ST. VAL. I knew your romantic and highly imaginative temperament—your belief in sylphs, guardian angels, and good fairies. Approach, my sylph.

Enter SPIRIT, R.

Behold your young Mentor, my pupil; he is the son of one of your courtiers, thus costumed and instructed, to appear before you as "The Spirit of the Wood," to present to you those flowers, and make you fancy they were in reality a talisman. Can you pardon me?

FLORI. You have given me a lesson which I trust I shall never forget. As to the young peasant, Andre, who told me the truth so soundly?

ST. VAL. Not being aware of your rank. I have seen him, explained to him who you were, and here he comes to thank you for your kind intentions.

Enter ANDRE, L.

FLORI. Well Andre, what is now your opinion of Prince Florimond?

ANDRE. (*falls on his knees*) Oh, your most excellent highness, do pray forgive me.

FLORI. What, for speaking out like an honest-hearted lad! Heaven forbid, that I should harbour one resentful thought towards those who have the courage to tell me of my faults. (ANDRE *rises*) Andre, I appoint you one of my head gardeners; and, poor as my exchequer may be at present, I can promise that sixty crowns shall be forthcoming to purchase a cow.

ANDRE. And I am to get all this for only speaking the truth!

ST. VAL. Yes; and let this be a lesson to those who need it. Truth is, indeed, a precious Talisman; and, as the proverb says——

SPIRIT. "Truth may be blamed: it can never be shamed."

Curtain.